LIVING PHILOSOPHY IN KIERKEGAARD, MELVILLE, AND OTHERS

LIVING PHILOSOPHY IN KIERKEGAARD, MELVILLE, AND OTHERS

Intersections of Literature, Philosophy, and Religion

Edward F. Mooney

BLOOMSBURY ACADEMIC
NEW YORK • LONDON • OXFORD • NEW DELHI • SYDNEY

BLOOMSBURY ACADEMIC
Bloomsbury Publishing Inc
1385 Broadway, New York, NY 10018, USA
50 Bedford Square, London, WC1B 3DP, UK
29 Earlsfort Terrace, Dublin 2, Ireland

BLOOMSBURY, BLOOMSBURY ACADEMIC and the Diana logo are trademarks of
Bloomsbury Publishing Plc

First published in the United States of America 2020
This paperback edition published in 2021

Copyright © Edward F. Mooney, 2020

For legal purposes the Acknowledgments on p. xiv constitute an
extension of this copyright page.

Cover design by Eleanor Rose
Cover image © Manuel Breva Colmeiro / Getty Images

All rights reserved. No part of this publication may be reproduced or
transmitted in any form or by any means, electronic or mechanical, including
photocopying, recording, or any information storage or retrieval system,
without prior permission in writing from the publishers.

Bloomsbury Publishing Inc does not have any control over, or responsibility
for, any third-party websites referred to or in this book. All internet addresses
given in this book were correct at the time of going to press. The author and
publisher regret any inconvenience caused if addresses have changed or sites
have ceased to exist, but can accept no responsibility for any such changes.

Library of Congress Cataloging-in-Publication Data
Names: Mooney, Edward F., 1941- author.
Title: Living philosophy in Kierkegaard, Melville, and others :
intersections of literature, philosophy, and religion / Edward F. Mooney.
Description: New York : Bloomsbury Academic, 2019. | Includes bibliographical
references and index. | Summary: "Unravels the philosophical, literary, and
personal theaters of faith, self-deception, communion, difficult reality,
and existential crisis in texts by Kierkegaard, Melville, Henry Bugbee,
and others."– Provided by publisher.
Identifiers: LCCN 2019025904 (print) | LCCN 2019025905
(ebook) | ISBN 9781501357718 (hardback) | ISBN 9781501357725 (epub) |
ISBN 9781501357732 (pdf)
Subjects: LCSH: Philosophy and religion | Kierkegaard, Søren, 1813-1855.
Classification: LCC B56 .M64 2019 (print) | LCC B56 (ebook) | DDC 100–dc23
LC record available at https://lccn.loc.gov/2019025904
LC ebook record available at https://lccn.loc.gov/2019025905

ISBN:	HB:	978-1-5013-5771-8
	PB:	978-1-5013-8312-0
	ePDF:	978-1-5013-5773-2
	eBook:	978-1-5013-5772-5

Typeset by Integra Software Services Pvt Ltd.

To find out more about our authors and books visit www.bloomsbury.com
and sign up for our newsletters.

Exultation is the going
Of an inland soul to sea,
Past the houses — past the headlands —
Into deep eternity —

~ Emily Dickinson

For Tami, as always

CONTENTS

Preface xi
Acknowledgments xiv

1 Passionate speech: Improvisations in the disorders of desire 1
2 The very tang of life: Lyrical jesting in Kierkegaard's *Postscript* title 9
3 Existentialism: Hardly navel-gazing 23
4 Henry Bugbee, religious philosopher 27
5 Melville: What philosophers learn at sea 43
6 Where is God?: Ahab at sea 53
7 Intimate communions 67
8 Who is Kierkegaard? 77
9 Kierkegaard, seduction, and circus identity 95
10 Difficult faith and living well 103
11 Faith can't be self-deceptive 111
12 Nurturing love 119

13 Socrates: Of woman born 129

14 Literature, philosophy, and existential contributions 141

Epilogue: Truths in the trenches 151

Notes 164
Bibliography 180
Index 183

PREFACE

Philosophy and religion can intensify or clarify a stance toward oneself, others, and the world. Narratives are often the vehicle. In a famous passage from Dostoevsky, Ivan Karamazov tells the story of the Grand Inquisitor to his younger religious brother Alyosha. The tale embeds an intersection of philosophy, religion, and literature, a powerful mix I find in Kierkegaard, Stanley Cavell, Melville, Henry Bugbee, and Wittgenstein. Narrative passages from these writers present deep thoughtfulness, veering toward the religious, and tuned to the moment. They are not pronouncements from eternity or timelessly valid demonstrations. They're dramatic, episodic and conversational, exposing felt-realities. "Living Philosophy" in my title has a double sense. We have *philosophy* that's conveyed as a dramatic living narrative. And second, we have a spectrum of persons who in various ways are *living out* their philosophies.

I consider writing that delivers a tang of life and moments of passionate speech, that displays the nature of circus identity. I take up matters of self and soul, acting and receiving, thought and passion. Kierkegaard is the first existentialist, and as such he stirs the fabric of daily life, its crises and communions, its joys and irony, its humor and grief. *Fear and Trembling,* Kierkegaard's great book, uncovers romantic and maternal love, self-deception and redemption, all with sharp wit and humor. Melville's *Moby-Dick* also stirs daily life, playing variations on death and rebirth, rage and affection. *The Book of Job,* the centerpiece of Henry Bugbee's stirring meditations, dramatizes the limits of justice and culminates in what Tennyson calls the greatest poem in all literature.

These accounts of grave and exuberant matters bring us beyond psychological, sociological, or commonsensical ways of understanding. They come to inhabit the soul. A soul is at the receiving end of things, a site of imaginative mulling and yielding, of listening that counters a self that seeks mastery. The worlds of Kierkegaard, Melville, or the author of *Job* value action and also cherish a yielding soul.

Kierkegaard invents new literary genres that test our tolerance for complexity and drama. Melville wields a Biblical and Shakespearean prose that opens passionate dialogue and soliloquy across divisions of class, race, and religion. We're drawn into uncharted territory. Familiar maps give way to improvised sketches as we seek our way. We are executive selves and equally diaphanous and vulnerable souls taken by terror, beauty, and the radiant commonplace. Philosophy, faith, and literature come together. Religion and literature become philosophical and philosophy leaves the ivory tower. Literary philosophers like Montaigne, Thoreau, Nietzsche or Cavell seek episodic *felt-realities*. What unfolds is not assured knowing or a philosophical system but the exaltation or terror of an open sea. Perhaps we uncover Ishmael's "eternal mildness of joy."

I begin with Stanley Cavell, whose *"passionate speech"* realigns the paths of personal desire. Then I trace a zest for life in the full title of Kierkegaard's *Concluding Unscientific Postscript*. Gordon Marino's *Existentialism: Being Authentic in an Inauthentic Age* is the focus of Chapter 3. *The Book of Job* gives us Job's closing confession, "I knew not whereof I spoke," the framing motif of Henry Bugbee's meditations. Chapters 5 and 6 trace *Moby-Dick's* twists and turns through the actions, passions, and abdications of Ahab, Ishmael, and others. We discover episodic, conversational philosophies, and startling moments of faith.

In "Intimate communions," and in "Who is Kierkegaard?", Chapters 7 and 8, I explore Kierkegaard's brilliant, amusing, and difficult *oeuvre*. "Kierkegaard's Seductions and Circus Identity" unravels my own close-up responses to reading Kierkegaard. "Difficult Faith and Living Well" argues that Kierkegaard's faith needn't diminish goods offered by secular life; and "Faith and Self-Deception," Chapter 11, shows that true Kierkegaardian faith makes self-deception impossible. Nurturing love is central in *Fear and Trembling*: Chapters 12 and 13 follow Socrates' need of a woman to know love: he makes Diotima his trusted expert. And I suggest why philosophers have sidelined maternal love. "Philosophy, Literature, and Existential Contributions" takes Henri Bergson's resolution to wear a Star of David in Nazi-occupied Paris to exemplify an existential stand. I conclude with an epilogue, "Truths in the Trenches," defending the domain of subjective, existential truths.

The rough form of these chapters originally saw the light of day as responses to particular audiences. As I deliver them here, especially in the Kierkegaard chapters, there will be repetition of framing facts and presuppositions. This assists new audiences needing orientation. This also means that it is unnecessary to read these chapters in the order they are presented here.

I had no master plan for a book, only the compulsion to join conversations begun in my readings. I found myself responding intimately to particular texts and themes. This is not the outcome of a research project but essays along paths that only gradually revealed their interweaving. For me, this traces a life's work. It aims at the sort of exaltation sketched by Emily Dickinson on my title page, "the going of an inland soul to sea."

ACKNOWLEDGMENTS

Each chapter below is a response to a friendly invitation by a good colleague. These include Dana Lloyd, Tami Yaguri, Kelly Dean Jolley, Dan Conway, Rev. Andrew Brown, John Davenport, Bruce Kirmmse, Steve Webb, Gary Whited, George Pattison, Gordon Marino, Corey McCall, Eric Ziolkowski, and I'm sure a few others. Supportive colleagues are a special audience and indispensable for my writing.

I'd also like to acknowledge my supportive new family in Portland, Maine: KE, Paul, DD, David, Ellen, Landis, and Dominique. Last but not least, thanks to the wonderfully cheerful staff at Hilltop Café that set me going each morning at 9:00 with an excellent large cappuccino. Thanks, too, to the calming serenity of Casco Bay.

Let me also acknowledge the rich blessings of a long and varied life that make meditation on such matters as I pursue here possible and deeply rewarding.

1
Passionate speech: Improvisations in the disorders of desire

I'll let Kelly Dean Jolley set the stage for a retrieval of passionate speech, as it's found in poetry and elsewhere, and as it connects to mystery and the folds of the soul.

> We have become secular people, partial people; we no longer believe in, much less live in the interpenetration of the natural and the supernatural: we have lost that sense of mystery that creates ceremony, that reveals to us the garden of the world we live in. In our loss of that sense of mystery, we have lost what galvanizes us against sloth, prevents our souls from growing woolly and fungous … Blind to the seasons' gifts, numb to nature … careless of ourselves and of others, bored alike by damnation and salvation, we become graceless by inaction. It is one (one) aim of poetry to recover that sense of mystery, to beckon us from sloth.[1]

Here's a plaque from the foot of Mt. Washington, a great *instance* of passionate speech.

> CAUTION: The appalling and needless loss of life on this mountain has been due largely to the failure of robust trampers to realize that wintry storms of

incredible violence occur at times even during the summer months. Rocks become ice-coated, freezing fog blinds and suffocates, winds of hurricane force exhaust the tramper, and when he stops to rest, a temperature below freezing completes the tragedy. If you are experiencing difficulty, abandon your climb! The highest wind velocities ever recorded were attained on Mt. Washington. Since the worst is yet to come, turn back without shame, before it's too late.[2]

Stanley Cavell would call this passionate speech. It gets under my skin; it invades my psyche in the area of my shames and prides and fears. It "improvises in the disorder of my desires."[3] Should I go on up the trail, not yet icy—or turn back? That might seem like a straightforward practical question to be settled by experts—perhaps I should ask a park guide. Yet it's not hard to imagine that this CAUTION brings me into Dante's dark woods where the troubled soul is exposed, where a simple caution drifts toward a sort of life-crisis: how do I handle this challenge—who will I be, or become, in meeting, or fleeing it?[4]

Care for the soul moves in different terrain than care for the self. The self takes on executive initiatives, has critical and rational drives, and has a will to take charge of life and master its obstructions—"just do it." Care for the soul is something else again. To value the soul is to be open to one's deepest passion, its capacity to value. As W. E. Hocking puts it, to care for the soul is to "prize the personal center of caring, the heart."[5] It is to yield to and care for the untamed, the irresolvable or intractable, the realm of conflicting shadows. David Rothenberg captures the risks: "There is something dangerous about the grooves that capture the soul. They pull us in and there is no escape."[6]

Why should a trailhead warning strike me as an address to my soul—rather than an innocuous traffic sign: "*Danger: Bump ahead!*"? No doubt it's about grappling with shadowy, exciting, and dangerous challenges. Life and death then appear as a symphony of thrills, falls, threats, and vast vistas. Perhaps this CAUTION is a reminder of my finitude. The majestic and sublime can be supremely indifferent to my well-being, despite the self's will-to-mastery. A sharp reminder of finitude, the failure of mastery in death, calls me to a piety I've abandoned. It addresses me in an idiom not solely secular.

Against detachment

I inhabit a typical secular university. Despite my invocations of the sacred or the soul, I doubt I'll be called before academic inquisitors. If I were, the indiscretion would be my trespass on private property. I'd be taking from the selves in my charge their executive privileges, their right to be masters of their thoughts. This is a prerogative of priests but not of professors. In my appeal to regions of their souls, I am disrespecting the sanctity of our shared secular calling. My students seek simple knowledge or skills in critique—not transformation of soul. I touch on gods, prophecy, or piety, not just in an abstract theoretical way, but by letting reverence and prophecy touch down in the class. This passionate text at the foot of Mt. Washington is reproduced as I read it with passion, making my classroom a place for pious souls, not just for secular selves. It intrudes on the privacy of an innocent listener, that one, in the second row.

If I were asked collegially what piety and soul were doing in a secular classroom, I could ask in return why I should stick with a valorization of the secular that excludes evocations of piety. After all, I didn't hold a church service but exposed a piety half-concealed in an otherwise fully secular trailhead CAUTION. And I could ask why in this age of dark woods and horrors, questioning the limits of the executive self violates the aims of the humanities.

Literature, philosophy, art, religion, and music—the humanities—are portals to all things human, and piety is one of those things. There's truth in piety's reticence, patience, and listening. It's relief from relentless self-assertive critique. In teaching, I move naturally from a mountain-trail CAUTION or a poem of Emily Dickinson to contemplative activities, such as reading, writing, thinking quietly, focused on texts tilted toward the religious.[7] These words are prophecy: "*The Worst Is Yet to Come! Turn Back without Shame!*"

Passion, the soul

A prolific man of letters and elegant philosopher, Stanley Cavell takes "passionate utterance" to mark the place where soul is at stake. Passionate utterances are "invitations to improvisation in the disorder of desire."[8] He doesn't cite the CAUTION posted at White Mountains trailheads. That's my "art trouvè" that sets me improvising on mortality and hubris, shame and self-assertion, piety and impiety. Cavell links passionate speech to "redemptive writing" and "redemptive reading."[9] Souls, not selves, need redemption.

We can find witness to "passionate speech," witness to souls in dark woods, in the epigraph to Cavell's signal 1962 article, "The Availability of the Philosophy of the Later Wittgenstein." He quotes Jean Giraudoux:

> Epochs are in accord with themselves only if the crowd comes into these radiant confessionals which are the theaters or the arenas, and as much as possible ... to listen to its own confessions of cowardice and sacrifice, of hate and passion ... For there is no theatre which is not prophecy. Not this false divination which gives names and dates, but true prophecy, that which reveals to men these surprising truths: that the living must live, that the living must die, that autumn must follow summer, spring follow winter, that there are four elements, that there is happiness, that there are innumerable miseries, that life is a reality, that it is a dream, that man lives in peace, that man lives on blood; in short, those things they will never know.[10]

Can a philosopher's solely rational analysis make anything of this? The words seem sermonic or acceptable only as poetry, far from levelheaded philosophy.

They appeared in the most poetry-averse of philosophical journals. Reading them in the 1960s was a breath of fresh air.

Mainstream philosophers have by and large disowned passionate speech. We teach critical thinking but not feeling attentively; we teach rational decision theory but not responsible passions. Many read the poetry of *Genesis* as botched evolutionary biology—as if ballet is a botched dash for the bus. Our blindness to the varied registers of biblical narration, ballet, and biology is both bad logic and stunted passion. Seeing better and feeling with more subtlety can mark metamorphosis of spirit. The worst of passions can be deflated by rational critique, but defeating the worst is not attaining the best.

The great novels of Henry James or George Eliot (among many others) show conversational and emotional exchange—mild passions—effecting change in persons and desires.[11] We arrive imaginatively at a more tempered, less imprisoning or explosive, set of passions. Here is George Eliot redeeming us not from sin but from a certain blindness.

> That element of tragedy which lies in the very fact of frequency, has not yet wrought itself into the coarse emotion of mankind; and perhaps our frames could hardly bear much of it. If we had a keen vision and feeling of all ordinary human life, it would be like hearing the grass grow and the squirrel's heartbeat, and we should die of that roar which lies on the other side of silence. As it is, the quickest of us walk about well wadded with stupidity.[12]

Is it tragic that our rhythms, our inhalations and exhalations, poorly match the rhythms of seas, seasons, or stars? Is it tragic that our breathing is manic relative to the breathing of oaks or the drift of clouds? Is it tragic that the stride of our walk is nothing compared to the stride of mountains? Should our heartbeats be more akin to those of the humming bird? Eliot raises unanswerable but haunting questions.[13]

Her words bring us to think on first and last things, the hallowed ground of the sacred. She reminds us that dull vision or numbness toward ordinary life is imprisoning. Salvation is better seeing, imagining, and feeling. If we opened to revelations of "quite ordinary" reality, we'd die on the spot from the sublime roar. Ethics can tell us what might release the good as well as tell us how to restrain the bad. A vision of the "frequency" of life might do this.

Pleadings and warnings

As Cavell has it, "passionate utterance" is speech neither purely descriptive nor the ceremonial or quasi-legal domain of performative utterance. To say, "freezing fog blinds and suffocates" might be construed as simply fact-stating. But at a trailhead it's a screaming CAUTION, not only informative but also a pleading and warning. It's urgently uttered from the heart, meant to *impact* my heart, realign my desires. It's meant to burn into the tramper's soul. It's meant to instill imaginative empathy with another tramper, one caught in mortal tragedy. It improvises pleadingly in the disorder of my desires.[14] Unlike the performative "I thee wed," uttered by a pastor in a ceremonial setting, it does not alter the social world. It has none of the force of a ranger's shout at close quarters: "Evacuate!" If I head back rather than continue, it's due to its elegant improvisation, not to overt threat or coercion or ceremonial effectiveness.

Giraudoux leads me to ask if my desires are disordered and distort my knowledge. I know and don't want to know that I'm cowardly, or will die, or that there is misery, or that man lives on blood. Passionate utterance invokes shapes of passion and desire, of imagination and sensibility, prompting the responsiveness Kierkegaard calls our subjectivity. Arcing words can lift us— or leave us indifferent. They live or die as we receive or refuse them. We might find them saving or banal: *"No man is an Island ..."*—*"The readiness is all ..."*—*"Let it be!"*—*"Ain't I a woman?"*—*"The unexamined life is not ..."*— *"I have a dream ... "*

I hear Hamlet's "Let it be!" or Donne's "No man is an Island" or Sojourner Truth's "Ain't I a woman?" and I am moved to iterations, and to critical and furthering comment, carrying the words forward in my own voice. These words (and mine) spread exponentially, broadening their echo spatially and temporally over an ever-widening community. They are proposals—invitational, intimate universals. They are lifelines—to grasp or not.

If philosophy infiltrates my passions, commitments, or desires—if it evokes passionate speech improvising in my soul—then it will not be lawyer-like argument, or analysis of social contracts, or debate about sense and reference. The exemplars of this wider sort of writing would include Rousseau's *Reveries of a Solitary Walker*, Kierkegaard's *The Point of View of My Work as an Author*, and Montaigne's *Essays*. Philosophy needs passion and song, for it is, after all, a love story. Love of wisdom means attention to the fine textures of lives. It means love of a form of life suited to oneself and to others, in the light of the good, in the light of a love and life one can affirm in passionate speech.

Work in the dark

We find passionate truths of self and soul affirmed in the writings of Bugbee, Melville, and Kierkegaard. Yet in times of mass death, in Haiti or Yemen, what is literature—or philosophy's passionate speech? At a different level, after the extinctions that have befallen Rwandans and Jews and so many others, how is human being to go on? If atrocities gut their landscapes, what is left for reviving future Jewish or Yemenite souls?

Henry James has a writer confess:

We work in the dark—we do what we can—
we give what we have.
Our doubt is our passion and our passion is our task.
The rest is the madness of art.[15]

We work in the dark reading certain passages from Melville or Kierkegaard. We wonder if *we* sense what *they* sense and wonder if it can illuminate our *own* dark woods. We submit to the madness, the slight mitigation, of art. There are moments in passionate writing when interpretation does not "go all the way down," where there is *no* space between words and their impacts. Presence leaps from the page the way wonders leap from the world, leaving enormous room for love of the world, for ongoing revelation, for suspension of doubts. Here is a taste of brie, a wince at sudden light, the flight of an ethereal hawk. At such moments digressive interpretations will miss the grounding tenors of life.

The poet's unclouded lyrical eye gives us presence. Glaring styles of representation and analysis, or those that take flight only at dusk, muffle the eloquent presence and passionate speech that calls philosophy, poetry, and religion into being.

2
The very tang of life: Lyrical jesting in Kierkegaard's *Postscript* title

Heidegger gives us a striking characterization of philosophy that places it squarely in the domain of passionate speech, among the folds of the soul: "Philosophy necessarily stands in the radiance of what is beautiful and in the throes of what is holy."[1] If the beautiful and the holy are part of the drama of life, we could say of a philosopher that he:

> is trying to write the drama of life as it is, with all the stage directions, to express, not only what the actors do, say, think, and feel, but also what they are expressing. If one could succeed, the result would be life itself, completely known. We would see why, we would understand—and also, we would feel the very tang of life itself.[2]

Is it plausible that Kierkegaard writes amidst the beautiful and the holy, and aims to deliver the drama of life?

Many think of Kierkegaard as opinionated and didactic, offering propositions like "Truth is Subjectivity," and raising questions like "Is there a teleological suspension of the ethical?" A contrarian and often a skeptic, he teaches that ever-so-many positions or propositions are untenable. He also gives us, in a positive vein, brilliant psychology and philosophy. Yet beyond saying or arguing one thing or another, his words stir the soul in special ways, in ways that are paradoxically both elusive and vividly present—in the way the beautiful or the sacred can be both radiantly present and strangely elusive. Much excellent philosophical writing is straightforwardly propositional and argumentative. Heidegger, for one, wants more from philosophy. He wants it to stand "in the radiance of what is beautiful and in the throes of what is holy." Kierkegaard would concur.[3]

The presence of words and delivery

Much of Kierkegaard's writing is a kind of theater. He tries "to express, not only what [his] actors do, say, think, and feel, but also what they are expressing *in* that doing, saying, thinking, and feeling."[4] I can be stirred by the presence of *what* actors "do, say, think, and feel"—and by their presence *in* saying, doing, thinking, or feeing.

The words of love have a presence as words alone—as bare words. And *in* speaking, my tone of voice, its rhythm and timbre, and my bodily rigidity or slackness, can express a presence— fear, say, or hesitation or wholeheartedness. A court stenographer takes down words of a tearful witness. The bare words, and these alone, read later, can have a tearful presence. But the stenographer can't convey the presence of *delivery*: the face of the witness; the tone, volume, and emotive modulations of the voice; the tightness of limbs betraying fear, excitement, or awkwardness. It's like hearing subtleties beyond notes in musical phrasing.

Similarly, words from my philosophy text can stir at two levels. I look for arguments and concepts relevant to an upcoming report and find myself sometimes moved by their eloquence. And occasionally these words (say, in Plato's dialogues) can have a nearly voiced tangible weight, impact, pitch, rhythm—even overtones, bite, softness, or volume. Not all philosophers want to have their words come alive in diction or delivery. Learning to write for a Law Review is atonal—businesslike, concise. Speaking before a jury or teaching is the opposite. To accept and convey both the presence of words and the presence of delivery is to live in what Wittgenstein calls the inexplicit "spirit" of writing.[5]

Texts like Kierkegaard's *Postscript* can express opinions or launch a debate. They can also *hum* like a chorister treading home from church, or *crackle* like the punch lines of a comic, or *shout* like an insecure Sunday preacher. Sometimes, as in the *Postscript's* full title, the presence of unfolding words can *crash*—and then gently *purr*—like waves at the beach. The hum and crackle give me a world in its presence, in its mysterious coming-to-be.

I ask you to let Kierkegaard's opinions and arguments be teleologically suspended, as it were. This lets the *presence* of words and of their delivery take center stage. We then access their "tang of life." The presence of words and delivery is not *more* important than questions, concepts, or arguments. Nevertheless, it can be *strikingly* important. Schopenhauer or Plato, Kierkegaard or Montaigne, convey presence and spirit. Like whispers or cries, an *exclusively* cognitive tracking of sentences recedes to let new vistas arise.

Life vs. knowledge

"The very *tang* of life itself" can arrive in the presence of bare words: "the world is full of wonder and terror." And I can be struck by the *presence*—even the *music*—of wonder and terror, "the tang of life" unfolding. In writing "the drama of life as it is," Bradley wants to convey "the tang of life itself," and also to make that tang *"completely known."* Heidegger and Kierkegaard will demur. To aim for *complete* understanding and knowledge is to aim for an unbecoming mirage rather than "*the radiance of what is beautiful and … the throes of what is holy.*" To aim for complete knowledge forestalls being swept up in terror or exaltation. "The tang of life itself" is not a piece of knowledge or understanding.

Kierkegaard goes deeper than the Kantian point that complete knowledge escapes us. To fixate on the quest for knowledge narrows being alive (in more than a medical sense). To be vibrantly alive is to be animated by the unknown. Sports fans and players are alive *because* the outcome of a good match, or the outcome of the present pitch, is radically unknown. The young man in Kierkegaard's *Repetition* yearns for love and is alive precisely *because* his future is unknown. He awaits his "thunderstorm," something beyond his ken that may never arrive. Abraham's thunderstorm is the Lord's demand for Isaac. He's shocked into painful aliveness, swept up into a future radically unknown.

Life is unfinished, poised on the cusp of the new. No picture of completely known life can be drawn for it would necessarily leave out the living artist doing the drawing—whose life proceeds forward, outside the picture.[6] We can follow the tang of life's *coming-to-be* by lingering with the comic, lyric, even *monstrous* title of what we know as "*Postscript*," or "*Concluding Unscientific Postscript.*" Unfolding the title gives us "a tang of life."[7]

Assistant professors can be content to limit their lectures or papers to argument, analysis, and exposition. They repress the philosophical import of a child's smile—or the terror of a tsunami. They assign study passages in *Postscript*. We should be stunned by the full title: *A Final Unscholarly Afterthought, a Sequel to Scraps of Philosophy: A Mimicking, Pathos-filled, Dialectical Compendium and Existential Provocation.*

What's in a title?

(1) For the sake of efficiency or cognitive mastery, we disable moments of wonder, jest, or terror. Disabling the visceral trembling and fear

of *Fear and Trembling* lets me approach the argument. Downsizing *Postscript*'s title clears the way for dispassionate analysis.⁸ The bravado of the full title ("*A Final Unscholarly Afterthought, a Sequel to Scraps of Philosophy...*") is pared down. We have "*CUP,*" or "*Postscript.*" Gradually reversing this minimalism gives us a crescendo, a tang of life, its moments of laughter and wonder, its flamboyant chutzpah:

(2) **CUP** or ***Postscript*** becomes ***Concluding Unscientific Postscript*** (or "*Concluding Unscholarly Addendum*").⁹ This stretches to become

(3) ***Concluding Unscientific Postscript to Philosophical Crumbs*** (or *Philosophical Fragments, Trifles, Tidbits,* or *Scraps*). And the title grows once again

(4) ***Concluding Unscientific Postscript to Philosophical Crumbs: A Mimic-Pathetic-Dialectical Compilation*** (mime, tragedy, and dialectics are mixed and compiled). Then we find an existential flavor

(5) ***Concluding Unscientific Postscript to Philosophical Crumbs: A Mimic-Pathetic-Dialectical Compilation: An Existential Contribution***

To unfold the title slowly replicates a musician's strategy in mastering a difficult passage. She works on the first phrase, then adds the next, until the whole passage appears in its full flowing presence. These elongations, heard slowly, raise the question of what sort of thing we hold in our hands. It's a book to file under the letter "K." Then it gradually morphs into a shockingly funny, annoyingly mischievous enigma:

(1) Why take seriously something avowedly *unscientific or unscholarly*?

(2) Can a true book be a follow up to *crumbs* of philosophy?

(3) Can *wisdom* be delivered in scattered crumbs?

(4) How can a book combine both *the mimicry of comedy* and *the pathos of tragedy*?

(5) How can *dialectical philosophy* be combined with *comedy and tragedy*?

(6) How can a *compilation* escape being only a hodgepodge or unruly stack?

(7) What is *an existential* contribution? (In 1851, "existential" is a coinage.)

The title goes against nature and in that sense is monstrous. Perhaps it's burlesque, or the work of a court jester.[10]

The impulse to reduce the title to a single word rests on convenience and buffers anxiety: the full title boggles the mind! To cut back disturbing presence, I'll say it's just a book with faded yellow cover called "*Postscript*." This erases the full title's cognitive-affective swerve, its ontological jest. Nothing could *possibly* be a "*Concluding Unscientific Postscript to Philosophical Crumbs: A Mimic-Pathetic-Dialectical Compilation: An Existential Contribution.*" We tame the provocation and sparkle by thinking, "it's just '*Postscript*.'"

Hannay offers us *Concluding Unscholarly Addendum to Philosophical Crumbs*.[11] "*Unscholarly Addendum*" suggests "inconsequential afterthoughts." "*Crumbs*" (or "trifles," "smidgeons") are inconsequential, too—remains falling from the table of a royal magician. Mimicry, miming, and jesting are theatrical; so is the pathos of tragedy. A *Mimic-Pathetic* work is theater. "Dialectic" seems squarely "philosophical," and so, not theater. But perhaps Johannes Climacus is a *philosophical* impresario *directing* the "mimic-pathetic" theater contrapuntally, dialectically, as comedy, tragedy, satire, and farce. This leaves him theatrical *and* dialectical.

Postscript radiates "*the tang of life*" through its compilation of theatrical scripts and scenarios. As a deeply affected spectator, I might come to an "existential" realization that I have become *more* than a mere onlooker, a dispassionate reader. There are demands, calls, and invitations in *Postscript* that challenge me. Existential provocations are woven into the ridiculously funny. The title might be slapstick—*An Unsystematic Appendix to Philosophical*

Smidgeons—targeting professors in general, or perhaps Hegel's "Scientific System," or the vanity of philosophy generally. The mockery might be self-referential. Parody and jest can both hide and reveal a jester's unwillingness to swim the currents of Christian life. Climacus differentiates *seeing* the truth from acting *in* the truth. He advances to the brink of commitment, then hesitates. Here, we recognize *ourselves*.

A disappearing author

In my attention to the presence or radiance of words I suspend biography and history. Yet I identify Kierkegaard as an author, even while turning away from biography. We appreciate many folk tales, ancient epics, pieces of architecture, snatches of tunes, while knowing nothing, or next to nothing, about the material conditions of their genesis. Creative power is evident despite our often knowing next to nothing about individuals responsible for a striking "tang of life." The mysteries of creation lie on the surface. To read Homer, I can do without biography but not without musical attunement. "*Sing in me muse, Sing of the man of twists and turns driven time and again off course.*" So opens *The Odyssey*.[12] Or think of Grimm's fairy tales. Surely, they're muse-inspired, but no author is present. Quite apart from biography and historical context, the spirits of creation sing through Kierkegaard's dramas, too.

Say a bottle holding an unsigned manuscript washes up on a beach. I can ask who wrote it, but I don't need to have an answer to appreciate it. Say I have a Renaissance painting of dubious provenance. Was it actually produced in Raphael's studio? How much of the brush work is his, and how much the work of his assistants? But the unfolding presence of a work doesn't raise questions of provenance—as if the mystery and radiance is only the puzzle of *who* laid brush to canvas or put pen to paper; of *who* wrote under pseudonyms or plagiarized. Citizen-Kierkegaard disappears while I'm immersed in genesis-unfolding. Unsigned bundles of words washed up on the beach, even if subsequently shown to be Kierkegaard's, are as radiant *before* being linked to a Danish author as they are afterward.

The mystery of creation-underway is a presence to linger with, not a problem to solve. Taking up a problem is often optional—whether to analyze a tidal surge, and sometimes non-optional—whether to check the map when I'm lost. But being taken by a thrilling musical phrase, or seduced by the jest of a title, is not a matter of choice. The abstractions of the mind–body problem can be taken up or put down. The thrill of a Bach cadence *hits us* or *doesn't*. When we're struck by the wondrous surface of Kierkegaard's words, the urge to explain or take academic notes is suspended.

As objective scholars we ask who authors Kierkegaard's pseudonymous *Postscript*. Is it Citizen-Kierkegaard, or is it Johannes Climacus, erstwhile resident of an imaginary landscape populated by assistant professors, cemetery visitors, and Socratic stand-ins? We can't check with Kierkegaard to see if *he* admits to being Climacus in disguise. Anyway, why trust what a master of disguises says about which disguises aren't *really* disguises? Climacus signs off as S. Kierkegaard in *Postscript*.[13] But why take that avowal as determinative, rather than a deceptive red herring? Happily, we can respond to the text's liveliness without a clue as to the text's "real" author. We can hear music without knowing the composer. If signed texts *and* pseudonymous ones are equally revelatory, we can stop with the revelations.

Kierkegaard wrote an *unscholarly*, unacademic *Postscript*. He didn't spend years on how Hegel or Luther matured. To enjoy Homer, I'm not required to show how oral tradition shaped *The Odyssey*. Yet I still refer to Homer or Hegel or Kierkegaard. I speak nonhistorically, nonempirically about them. "Hegel" or "Homer" will then refer to an *experiential presence*. The proper names stand for an elusive center of narrative power and imaginative brilliance that leaps from the pages at hand.

Rushdie: Effs of the ineffable

There are moments that elicit a gasp or exclamation, a silent or vocalized *"Wonderful! Wow!"* This is less cogitation than a moment of applause or astonishment. People vary in susceptibility to this exuberance-reflex. This matter is not trivial, for as one writer puts it, "our most vivid encounters with reality come in experiences that shatter our categories."[14]

Many things can evoke a reflex of wonder, terror, amazement, or surprise.[15] Here is Salmon Rushdie on five sorts of mysteries that trigger gasps of recognition:

> Five mysteries hold the keys to the unseen: the act of love, and the birth of a baby, and the contemplation of great art, and being in the presence of death or disaster, and hearing the human voice lifted in song. These are the occasions when the bolts of the universe fly open and we are given a glimpse of what is hidden; an eff of the ineffable. Glory bursts upon us in such hours: the dark glory of earthquakes, the slippery wonder of new life, the radiance of Vina's singing.[16]

What Rushdie calls "keys to the unseen," "effs of the ineffable," are a presence that provokes "a tang of life." *"These are the occasions when the bolts of the universe fly open and we are given a glimpse of what is hidden."* For a friend unmoved by what stuns me, descriptions or explanations are no substitute for direct access. I put her in the path of the ineffable rather than give her a tedious speech. Rushdie's mysteries—birth, acts of love, great art, the presence of death and disaster, heart-shattering song—hold common themes.

Presence counts: How do we know we're in love? What is so attractive about *this* Beethoven performance? The inquisitive and analytical mind arrives secondarily. Explanation is not our only value. I cherish the genesis of love or song as I access it moment by moment.

Mystery delivers inexhaustible value in the way a child's smile can be of inexhaustible value. Fact-seeking or analytical frames of mind shut the door on presence and are only part of life-underway. I don't need explanations for why I fall in love (though they might be available). The glisten of genius unfolding is seemingly "pulled from thin air." We find it unfurled on every other page in Kierkegaard's writing.

Dark matter: Rushdie mentions being in the presence of death and disaster as mysteries. Goya's "Horrors of War" mark a nadir of darkness. Kierkegaard's churchgoers need the dark awakening of Abraham climbing Moriah. At *impact*, death and disaster rule out affirmation or celebration. Yet disaster can leave an aching for what is lost—precious things, precious people, things worth holding in memory despite loss.

Shimmering first: Explaining is a digression from experiential impact. Moving too quickly to explain breaks the spell and risks explaining away. The prose on the wall beside a museum painting focuses on facts that can work *at the expense* of experiential impacts. A passage from Dostoevsky or Beethoven, or a child's smile or falling in love, can confound us as mysteries that defy explanation—not that explanations *can't* or *shouldn't* be offered, but radiant impacts survive well enough *without* them. Explaining a cellist's captivating phrasing is disastrous if the moment of wonder disappears in the process.

Ordinary and extraordinary: The mysteries Rushdie names can appear both commonplace and miraculous. What's so special about childbirth? It's part of routine for nurses and clerks in maternity wards. For morgue-workers, there's nothing special about death. Yet I trust we know there's also something hauntingly wondrous or terrible on occasions of death, song, or birth. These mysteries—love, birth, great art, death or disaster, and singing—involve visceral encounters: the humdrum disappears.

Double and multiple: Artists, writers, congregants, mothers, citizens, sons must have double vision, giving both facts and *presences*, both explanations and *stunned silence*, a space to arise. We *need* multiple vision. *What we* encounter—straight facts and shimmering presences—activates double vision. That I am here available to the radiance of a cellist's phrasing is an added wonder to the wonder of her playing. We need multiple angles of vision distributed temporally to take in the truths, the realities, of all that's available.

What is the text?

The unstable *Postscript* title stands in for the mystery of creation. The book is two pounds, packed with genius, and a mystery that "shatters our conventional categories." It's also in flux. The phrasing of the cello emerges about *here* in the musical line and completes its appearance a few seconds later, about *here*—then it's passed. The *Postscript* title's expansions and contractions are the emergence and retreat of a cellist's phrase. Read it as a single word, then let it swell from a single word, *Postscript*, into a 12- or 14-word mini-aria that will then disappear. A phrase from the cello can emerge and disappear like a genie rising from a bottle, to disperse as vapor. I can no more force the unfolding title into a bottle for repetition or cognitive-only distribution than I can get a genie back into its bottle.

I can arrest the title long enough to ask whether the English should read "*unscholarly*" rather than "*unscientific*"—should read "*Fragments*" rather than "*Crumbs or Trifles*." I can ask whether "crumbs" are Biblical, falling from the table of a rich man—whether philosophy *ought* to be crumbs or fragments rather than explanations, systems, and arguments. I can ask how philosophy can be *comic mimicry*, how it can be *tragic pathos*, whether this is the spot "*existential philosophy*" is born. I can ask whether this title is the work of Kierkegaard or the work of Johannes Climacus, whether Climacus is a genie climbing out of the earth, John the Climber, and whether "Kierkegaard" is as much a *nom de plume* as "Climacus."

Kierkegaard's distain, in *Postscript* for "assistant professors," is distain for those who stick to analysis or explanation and forget human impact. Here, Heidegger asks us to go behind the surface of writing. Referring to Hegel's *Phenomenology*, he writes:

> [H]ere as everywhere else in genuine philosophy—[the inner form] is not an addition which is meant for the literary connoisseur. Nor is the question that of literary decoration or of stylistic talent. Rather, its inner form [what I—EFM—call "presence"] is the inner necessity of the issue itself.[17]

Of *Postscript*, we could say that its inner form (satire, jest, irony, pathos) is not merely a literary addendum inessential to the proposition that truth is subjectivity. Presence delivered through jest or pathos exemplifies the felt-necessity of subjectivity. Heidegger goes on:

> For philosophy is, like art and religion, a human-superhuman affair of primary and ultimate significance. Clearly separated from both art and religion and yet *equally primary* with both of them, philosophy necessarily stands in the radiance of what is beautiful and in the throes of what is holy.[18]

Kierkegaard's writing has an "inner form" that is more than literary; it brings me the wonder of coming-to-be, and brings me next to the beautiful and holy, art and religion. Hearing the *presence* of creation brings us to "a human-superhuman affair of primary and ultimate significance."

"Assistant Professors" are bemired in single vision, content with argument, analysis, or exposition. They have no ear for "double vision" (presence and facts), or for the allure of a smile or the terror of a tsunami. They hold up *Postscript* and assign study passages. There's no time to be stunned by *Final Unscholarly Afterthoughts in 600 pages, a Sequel to Scraps of Philosophy: A Mimicking, Pathos-filled, Dialectical Compendium and Existential Provocation*.

The moment of wonder might be followed by a deferential desire for elaborations. They needn't destroy the moment. They can lay out second or third angles of vision—giving what Wittgenstein calls "perspicuous representations."[19] He learned from Kierkegaard—among other things—how one could give multiple pictures of the lay of the land, shuffling them rather than fixating on a single picture. This is better than submitting to skepticism ("too many angles defeat knowledge") and better than grasping *one* angle as surely correct.

Creativity, egoism, self-abnegation

Undergoing the immediate impact of creation-underway can displace my importance. Now, as I write, I *defer* to the majesty of something appearing, apparently, from *nowhere*. On the other hand, looking back on my work, I might be in awe: it is *I* who encounter a sentence of my making. It's *my* creation. Well, which is it? Am I a world-*creator* (as I write)—or, as I write, am I overcome by the *majesty of a world*? Focusing on the majesty of a world-written-out can make actual historical authors seem inessential. Kierkegaard's deferring to pseudonyms, or Climacus's revocation of authorship, can seem like self-abnegation.[20] Authorial disappearance is the flip side of boastful self-assertion. We shift between the writer as hero, as god-like in world-creation, and a world so magnificent the author disappears.

A Hassidic story tells us we carry two notes in our pocket. On the first is written "The world was made for me." On the second is written "I am dust and ashes."[21] Artists and writers are generative centers of worlds they create. The world is made for them because *they make it*. Kierkegaard shapes worlds with the tip of his pen. It takes egotism to create an off-hand throwaway title like *Philosophical Crumbs*, or the full fourteen-word *Postscript* title.

Yet writers also undergo self-abnegation. Kierkegaard keeps walking offstage to let his figures and pseudonyms speak on their own.[22] He thinks, "The world was made for me," and then, "I am dust and ashes." He is the epitome of self-assertion and the epitome of self-emptying self-sacrifice. *The Odyssey*, Lascaux paintings, or Acadian fiddle tunes are anonymous. We *submit to their allure*. There are no heroically self-assertive creators. To follow the mimicking-tragic-carnival of *Postscript* requires multiple vision. We're gripped by this sideshow, then that.[23] The author is out of the way. These are miracles and mysteries in the sense that laws of nature or explanatory schemes become beside the point—not for all time, but for the instant of allure or repulsion. And for any full life, these moments are essential: "Our most vivid encounters with reality come in experiences that shatter our categories."[24]

In a sense it's a miracle that you and I are here at all—that we exist! We matter, and that puts us one by one at the center of the universe. We know simultaneously that each of us can *also* seem as *nothing*. Thus, it is with the neglected music of *Postscript's* full title. It presents a full "tang of life"—and then can disappear, a vapor or dust.

3
Existentialism: Hardly navel-gazing

In the 1950s, existentialism was a hot topic of cultured conversations; William Barrett's *Irrational Man* and Walter Kaufmann's *Existentialism from Dostoevsky to Sartre* were best sellers. There were voices for and against in the *Partisan Review* and *The Village Voice*. Existentialism was a mood as much as a philosophy, feeding on the ennui of the postwar years. This was an age of quiet desperation and existential angst, peopled by the hollow men, the faceless crowd, the man in a gray flannel suit.

By the mid-1960s, however, the mood was shifting from quiet desperation to public protest. In 1969, *The New York Review of Books* featured essays on Bobby Seale, Nixon's war machine, the battle of Berkeley, and a Yippee piece by Jerry Rubin. As a cultural presence, existentialism was now overrun by the anger stirred by the Vietnam War, Civil Rights movement, and Black Power; it was then that the Weather Underground came into existence. The cachet of existentialism also declined in Europe, for parallel reasons: "deconstruction" advanced, and Emmanuel Levinas replaced Camus as the cultural figurehead. Dallying with meaning in life, personal morality, or faith was now a pastime for the effete.

Gordon Marino's brilliant *The Existentialist's Survival Guide: How to Live Authentically in an Inauthentic Age* is a rendition of the themes memorably presented by Barrett and Kaufmann. Marino gives existentialism a twenty-first-century presence more gripping, nuanced, and convincing than in its initial American portrayal sixty years earlier. The personal may be the political, as activists claim, but it is also the richly existential, and it is fundamental in its own terms. It is hardly navel-gazing or a preoccupation of the clinically depressed. The author's compendious scholarship shines. As important for an existential account of the subject, Marino honors its deeply personal appeals, and he is adept at giving witness to fragments from his own rich personal history. Despite existentialism's decades in the shadows, no one cracking this book can think it is passé.

The chapters course through anxiety, depression, despair, and death, and into the recuperative light of authenticity, faith, morality, and love. The prose is electric, illustrating the point that existentialism is also literary; Rilke and Ralph Ellison make cameo appearances, just as we find here the compelling drama of Dostoyevsky's *Notes from Underground* and Tolstoy's *The Death of Ivan Ilyich*. The discussions are the best among dozens I've read over many years.

Marino places Kierkegaard and Nietzsche, Camus and Sartre center stage. The gaps between psychology and philosophy are closed. From the 1960s onward, Erich Fromm, Rollo May, and Erik Erikson, among others, kept the spirit alive, casting anxiety and its mitigation in terms borrowed from Sartre or Nietzsche. Marino continues this tradition, giving us Kierkegaard, Nietzsche, Camus, and Sartre at their eloquent and insightful best.

Is anxiety a mental disease calling for medical treatment, pharmaceutical, or otherwise? Marino gives us a chapter-length discussion. Perhaps it's a necessary, even welcome, aspect of the human condition. Kierkegaard identified anxiety as central to any identity worth the name. It rises to a high pitch when we ask: "How can I be the person I truly am and should be?" To have anxiety here shows I take my life seriously. In *Fear and Trembling*, Kierkegaard asks: Is Abraham's faith obedience to God? Gratitude that God delivered Isaac in Sarah's old age? Thanks, that God returns Isaac? How can Abraham believe in a God who at whim both gives and takes back? These are apocalyptic anxieties, putting God, woman, and man at great risk.

By steering through issues that bear on us personally, and revealing their disruption and augmentation of his life, Marino avoids purely abstract, academic exposition. Classes in existentialism and existential psychology are popular because, apart from vocational promises, they offer a personal relevance all too absent in lectures devoted solely to impersonal facts and techniques. While Marino's grasp of the literature is impeccable, his verve and wit as a writer stand out, and his self-revelations are not self-promotions.

"Authenticity" has a positive ring, but we may stumble trying to get clear about it. Marino helps clarify the terrain. Tolstoy's *The Death of Ivan Ilyich* is about authenticity and love, as well as death and dying. We witness the closing struggles of a man whose life, as he sees it now, was never more than "fitting in," "looking good"—getting promoted, getting a wife. At death's door he realizes he has never given warmth or an ounce of himself. He has been loving toward no one; his assembled relatives are strangers to him. Only his servant is kind, recognizing his master's fear and trembling, his struggle for words of contrition as time runs out. Ivan Ilyich cannot speak from the heart because he has never engaged his heart.

Marino asks us to move from deathbed vigils to death more generally. This ought to be simple enough. Objectively, death is all around me, no more elusive than the weather or taxes. Things change when a loved one or neighbor dies; to pause with their demise is often a poignant moment to assess the meaning of their lives. Battlefield deaths, murders, or suicides are more troubling to grasp. If death is universal and commonplace, how can it shake us to the core? From the inside, it casts into sharp and often painful relief what we care about. From the outside, it's no more interesting than the pedestrian fact that insects are squashed, or birds fly into glass.

And what of faith, that classic repository of meaning in life, of valorized compassion, of balms for anxiety and fear of death, of hope for new life?

Marino suggests there's an existential inescapability of faith-as-trust, theistic or otherwise, that survives despite declines in church membership and the polemics of "the New Atheists." Faith is a passion, not a litany of facts, and we can credit existentialists with the insight that eliminating moods and feelings from our self-understandings will also eliminate courage, hope, a sense of right and wrong, and a sense of personal resolution.

A full life I can call my own is not derivative, and it will ferry dark moods and also celebrations and loves, moral courage and kindness. If there's a place for anger and moral outrage, there's also a place for good-heartedness and neighbor-love. Attention to existential dimensions of living, and full incorporation of them, is not a devotion to systematic knowledge and technical analysis. It's acknowledging and sharpening our sensibilities to the moods and agitations we live with willy-nilly. We get a feel for them through philosophy, music, art, and literature. They stretch and refine our sensibilities. To acknowledge the varieties and vagaries of anxiety and meaning, of courage, authenticity, and compassion, is at the heart of any existentialist portrait of what it means to be human, and is at the heart of this *Survival Guide*.

4
Henry Bugbee, religious philosopher

The Harvard professor W. V. O. Quine called him "the ultimate exemplar of leading an examined life."[1] Albert Borgmann, a colleague of Henry Bugbee at the University of Montana, identifies two towering works in twentieth-century American philosophy. The first is John Rawls's *A Theory of Justice*; the second is Henry Bugbee's *The Inward Morning: Philosophical Exploration in Journal Form*.[2]

Royce and James are household names in American philosophy. Bugbee is relatively unknown. Like Thoreau before him, he was always more than a scholar and teacher. He was committed to living a spiritual-philosophical life. For him, philosophy is not a technical research discipline but an unending exploration of life—of *his* life and its place among other lives and among beings of nature. Professional prominence mattered little. Paramount was living philosophically—even religiously. His writing is often lyrical, letting life sing its multiple sufferings and joys. In many ways Bugbee is Thoreauvian. This happy intermingling of thought, living, and writing is in stark contrast with the Anglophone philosophical style that began to dominate the post–Second World War era: something dryly professional, technical, and irrelevant to the spiritual and personal lives of its practitioners or others.

Early life

Born February 19, 1915, in New York City, Bugbee received his BA in philosophy from Princeton in 1936. He rather fearlessly submitted "In Demonstration of the Spirit" as an honors thesis. He started graduate work in philosophy in California at Berkeley, where he intended to study aesthetics. His writing always engaged literary narratives, including scriptural narratives. For him, reason-only expositions were secondary. His graduate work was interrupted by Pearl Harbor. He joined the Navy, serving as captain of a minesweeper in the Pacific.

After the War, Bugbee returned to Berkeley, completing a PhD in 1948 under Jacob Loewenberg. Its fearless title was "The Sense and Conception of Being." Hired initially by Stanford, he was quickly called to Harvard, where he taught from 1948 to 1954. He was denied tenure. He had no interest in writing strictly professional essays. He took a year off to draft *The Inward Morning: A Philosophical Exploration in Journal Form*. This was in the tradition of Gabriel Marcel's *Metaphysical Journals* and Thoreau's *Journals*, two writers he deeply admired. Later, he would introduce Marcel, an urbane Parisian, to broad expanses of the Rocky Mountain West. *The Inward Morning* opens with a preface from Marcel and proceeds to recount childhood memories of woods and swamps, gripping war experiences, and wilderness treks in the Canadian Rockies. After leaving Harvard in 1954, he put down roots among Montana's Bitterroot Mountains where he taught philosophy and humanities at the University of Montana from 1957 to 1977. He died in Missoula in December 1999.

A philosophical sea change

American philosophy underwent a radical change in the years of Bugbee's productivity. He became a voice apart. Few knew how to listen. He was at home with the Americans James, Royce, and Hocking, but this era expired after 1945. A new style emerged in the 1950s and 1960s—the British analytical style embodied by Russell, Moore, and Ryle. The new American brand was led by Quine, C. I. Lewis, Carnap, and Putnam. This sort of philosophy aspired to the clarity and decisiveness of math and science. It lacked the reflective, unfinished personal intimacy that Bugbee so valued. For him, philosophy was meditative, a dialogical endeavor rather than argumentative or didactic. He took leads from Shakespeare, Thoreau, and Zen rather than from the logic of Quine, Russell, or Moore. He was unimpressed with competitive intellectual styles. He sought reflective insight, a day at a time.

Published in 1958, *The Inward Morning* was hailed by Huston Smith as "the most Daoist western book I know."[3] Others called it "a uniquely American existentialism," and a "lyrical philosophy." Despite contrary philosophical aspirations, Quine remembered Bugbee as "the ultimate exemplar of the examined life." Albert Borgmann remembered "a humanist par excellence" devoted to "the great literature of the West and the East" who "lived with and out of those texts."[4] Over the years Bugbee's wrote on Marcel, the *Book of Job*, wilderness, the sublime, love, and education. None of this was of mainstream interest. He sought the sacred and revelatory in texts and wilderness, and sought to embody their lessons.

Early writing

Bugbee's undergraduate philosophy thesis from Princeton, "In Demonstration of the Spirit," takes its title from 1 Corinthians 2:4: "My message and my preaching were not with wise and persuasive words, but with a demonstration of the Spirit's power."[5] It's startling that philosophers at Princeton sponsored and passed a thesis that invoked Biblical verse advising against rational persuasion and wisdom. Bugbee's genius, I suspect, was apparent, and his sponsors gave him slack. Even at this early stage, Bugbee refused to construe philosophy as providing a solely technical, cognitive grip. He rejects what Corinthians disparagingly calls "wise and persuasive words." He writes from a spiritual calling rather than from academic protocols. Bugbee's bibliography lists, of all things, the classical recordings that he reports were essential in feeding his spirit. Without this music, he says, the thesis would not have been possible. Even more astonishing, the last word of the thesis is a handwritten "Amen." Has this been a prayer? Or a sermon? This is no standard undergraduate philosophy thesis.

Bugbee's handwritten "Amen" seals his anomalous wedding of the philosophical and the religious. He doesn't *argue* that prayer and liturgy are deeper than reasoned analysis can ever be. And this is not an undergraduate blunder. The writing is impressively mature. Bugbee knows he is not writing within a seminarian community. He knows he challenges the presumptions of a secular university. His title, benediction, and musical acknowledgments abandon us in an anomalous zone where philosophy and scripture, wisdom and revelation, spirit and reason, intermix. The thesis violates a taboo. Academic philosophy can't be mixed with confessional, religious meditation. This is a kind of civil disobedience—knowingly breaking a law to make a deep spiritual point. Bugbee's chapters on art and religion unfold appropriately for academic readers, yet they lie side by side with the closing "Amen," and with the opening biblical quotation. A taboo is broken in the name of a forgotten spirit in philosophy, a spirit that walked with the Divine.

On Job

Decades after his dissertation, Bugbee continues a mix of philosophy and religion. "A Way of Reading the Book of Job" is philosophical reflection *and* religious meditation. It displays Bugbee's reflective poetic prose, and his uncanny ability to be simultaneously philosophical, literary, and religious.

We know the abysmal suffering. Job's afflictions strike, round after round. In short order, he loses fortune, family, health, and friends—"friends" who recoil in fear and self-righteous judgment. They peer or burst out with blame. Job counterattacks. He demands that the LORD give him reasons for his pain.

Job presumes—falsely, it turns out—that God has an *ultimate* concern for Justice. True, Job's worldly goods are returned twofold. But a restitution of assets can't make up for the suffering. If I burn my neighbor's house, I can't be vindicated by building a replacement double the size. And Job is *not* demanding restitution. He wants to know *why* God afflicts him. That question isn't answered. God is neither just nor unjust, and Job can't be bought off by a Divinity bequeathing assets—hush money.

In Bugbee's retelling, the tale is like a dream. Job receives neither reasons nor justice but the great song of the Whirlwind, the song of creation: wonders of seas and storms, of leviathan, soaring hawks and dawn. In what Tennyson calls the greatest poem in literature, we see Job stunned, aghast—quiet before creation's multitudes. He's quieted by a new openness to the world's grandeur. He yields to a profound appreciation of magnificence: living creatures, great storms, ragged mountains, oceans of stars. He's humbled by a majesty that takes his breath away: *"I knew not whereof I spoke; I retreat in silence."*[6]

Job's question, "Why me?" disappears. A justice-ruled world is replaced by a spiritually sublime world. The storm opens sacred dimensions that his suffering (and demand for reasons) had darkened. Awe-filled silence replaces lawyer-like attacks. Resentment or complaint recede. Job is swept up in an abundant, terrifying existence *beyond* justice or reason: *this* soaring hawk, *this* fearsome leviathan, *there ... just there!*

Bugbee's meditative account opens in an unstudied voice—the tone of the tavern storyteller, sharing a yarn with a friend.

It came to me as in a dream, and it has that kind of logic, you know. Something about God and Satan and a man named Job. He got a rough deal, but then that's nothing special.

This is the idiom and tone of the village. He's not talking down from an academic or pastoral podium as a member of a learned elite.

The story is dream-like, begging for interpretation the way strange dreams do. "What is the *meaning* here?" Bugbee recounts the catastrophes, the abandonments by friends and wife, the near defeat of morale. Then the action stalls. There's a pause, as if Bugbee is sitting quietly with Job. Job has reached a dead-end. Both are quiet. Neither abandons the other.

Meditative drift

Days later, Bugbee begins again. Now his thoughts appear as if from a journal with dated entries. They are unhurried, spread out over time yet with a great specificity of place. Dreams are timeless but require intervals for interpretation to marinate. Philosophical arguments may have timeless validity, but they abandon the ups and downs of the heart. The abstracted writer becomes disincarnate, beyond place, mood, or voice. But Bugbee has heart, mood, and place voiced. Here is the first entry in its entirety.

Tuesday, January 15, 1963

No wind stirs. At Zero Fahrenheit the flakes of snow are not at all large. Incredibly lightly and unwaveringly they fall. A myriad of them fills our meadow round the house. One sees them best looking at the trees beyond. Their falling accentuates the still-standing trees, the dark trunks. And the still of the trees is the nearness of falling snow.

Occasionally, in the meadow, a weed nods and lifts again.

The low fire on the hearth is even more discreet.

The academic, critical, or reason-seeking mind is quiet. This is like a dream. We expected a commentary, but the story of Job seems shelved. The reflective, poetic entries seem eerily disconnected from Job or his plight. Yet the evocation of snow, of fire on the hearth, of still-standing trees, is surely Job's quiet.

This showing-of-things-happening embodies a patient readiness and receptivity. Poetry welcomes meadow and falling snow, the steadiness in snow, in a hearth's warmth, in trees seen through snow. We are visited by the nod and lift of a weed. This is a miniature of Job's whirlwind visitation. Job's present moment is ours.

We absorb the wonder of snow falling against still-standing trees and Job's patience, free of restless worry or disquiet. Discretion refuses to jump judgmentally to outrage or condemnation. Job had only the warmth from his dung heap; we have a low hearth fire. Our distance from his afflictions doesn't mar a willingness to be with him, sit with him. Bugbee incarnates poetical-spiritual-attention, patience with scripture, and Job, and falling snow.

Patience abides

Nearly a month later, a second journal-like entry is added. Apparently in matters of the spirit, there is no great rush for answers.

Tuesday, February 12, 1963

No great pressure of anything to say. No salient point to be made. No sureness about what might need to be done. Doubt with respect to so much of past thought. A sense of turning away from overstatement, a reticence almost to speak at all. Yet—perhaps even when so situated, some things need to be said, await being discovered in a way of saying them, if one were only to try it patiently and unassumingly enough, beginning over and again just with what offers itself. [I]t might even be as well to set out from a sustained reticence to speak. For whatever there may be amiss in it, that reticence also seems attuned to the quiet of heaven-and-earth, the unprejudiced silence of things that are, companioning an unlonely solitude. Not a life apart or solitary, but such solitude as heaven-and-earth dispense, to which one may give himself. Surely silence and solitude may be a measure for our thought and speech. And since by this measure we are simply placed on our own as well, it is a measure that also makes for reflection, and a finding out of what we make of things, in the course of having to do with them. In a mortal life.

Bugbee works to make out—and show through his words—the meaning of reticence, solitude, mortality, tentativeness, silence. Each is proper in approaching this scripture. There's no place for rapid-fire classroom analysis, no preacher booming admonitions, no philosopher laying down proofs.

Bugbee's reticence, patience, and solitude in writing duplicate Job's as he yields to the Whirlwind's magnificence—and then silently accommodates its transformative lesson. He works seamlessly with his text as partners work seamlessly in common tasks with no need for flourishes—only steady attention to the task, and quiet awareness of we who are present.

Dated entries mark a day's labor. The harvest is sentences, unmistakably his, delivered from a particular life, at a particular time and season, from a particular place. He places us to sense that the voice of things is heard only as we listen from a place of quiet, say, looking out over a meadow, a place of reticence and mortality.

From Job's being, from Bugbee's being, the Whirlwind draws out something akin to wavering grass or still falling snow. There's something deeply impersonal in our being-with-things and their being-with-us. Each lets the other be. Things-happening—snow, grass—are not here to win us over nor do they monitor our personal life. Job is addressed as one among many in a panoply of glorious yet impersonal creation. Bugbee puts it this way:

> At the core of personal life there seems to be something inviolately impersonal, akin in our fashion to the mode of being of rose, or rock—known and owned by all weather. It is through this in us that the elements

seem most deeply to befriend us—sun and rain, earth and seasons, the constant rivers and the starry night. It is through this that one may "go and come with a strange liberty in Nature, a part of herself." And it is this as well which may ground and fortify both critical reserve and human warmth: something inviolately impersonal. Perhaps it was to this that Job was led.

Inviolate presence of things

To be inviolate is to be immune from meddling—to be primal, serene, radiant, even wild. After the Whirlwind's retreat, Job is instilled with quiet understanding: things do not revolve around him, his catastrophes or triumphs. Opening to the meadow and falling snow is opening to inviolate presence. Bugbee sidelines Job's early complacent prosperity and later afflictions, protest and near-despair. He aligns to Job's final quiet receptivity.

> If we turn to the vision actually set forth in the utterance of the voice from the whirlwind, perhaps we must distinguish between the thread of argument intertwined with it and what actually emerges as to be seen, co-articulate with the mode of vision enacted. Simply, it is a vision of things: the things of heaven-and-earth, dramatized in their emergent majesty, wonder, and inviolable reserve. But seen in the mode of this, their being. And seen as if for the first time, yet as belonging to a domain, in which dominion (not domination) reigns, forever and ever: the domain of being itself.
>
> Job's questioning has presupposed an explanation of things and events; he has believed in a justice embodied in them, but in a way suggesting the possibility of a *raison d'être* through which comprehension of them would be the appropriate mode of understanding with regard to them.
>
> But his presupposition does not seem to be sustained; rather, it is shown to be irrelevant. No explanation of what has befallen him is forthcoming;

certainly not any "justification of human suffering." In fact, nothing by way of justification conceived on the model of moral persuasions occurs. No hidden purposes are revealed, to disclose that these, then, explain, or exemplify how explanation might be forthcoming, to whatever extent withheld. Instead, wanting to understand as he does—with his whole heart—and at his wits' end, prepared to risk whatever in his belief he may have clung to, Job is opened in mutual address with things. And the vision enacted speaks, not according to his presuppositions. Nevertheless, it speaks in recognition of his situation and condition. His belief in *raison d'être* [in things having a reason for being] is strangely and wonderfully both controverted and confirmed: *L'être-meme, c'est la raison*. Their very being itself is their reason for being. But therefore: no *raison d'être*. [Angelus Silesius: "*La rose est sans pour quoi.*" The rose is without a reason why—it just is.] Thus, it is in a certain appreciation of things, in a relation of mutual address with them, and not in any comprehension of them, that a basic mode of understanding comes to pass.

Understanding does not fulfill philosophy's promise of secure cognitive grasp but comes to pass "through a glass darkly." To be by the hearth and see the nearness of snow etched against trees is not philosophical knowledge or explanation but a *reception-of-happenings*, happenings that deliver revelatory understanding. Philosophy becomes poetic:

> Canst thou command the dawn?
> Like clay, the shape of things is changed by it;
> They stand forth as if clothed in ornament! (Job 38: 12–15)[7]

Job listens and is overwhelmed—not as a stronger force overwhelms an enemy or reduces others to servility. He is overwhelmed as great music overwhelms, sweeping aside our will and power. Yielding to music makes space for truths that escape words:

It was music which first awakened me to the need for reflection; but for the music which aroused and defined a sense of unconditional reality in me, I doubt if I would have found it relevant to reflect on our condition in a way that drew me to the works of philosophers.[8]

Music instills a sense of reality. Like the reality of dawn, it dresses the day. Job opens to dawning appreciations. Music pushes back the dark, as a musical Whirlwind does.

Job is informed by the gift of an aesthetic-religious epiphany. He's addressed by a world replete with magnificent living things, inviolate things-happening and inviolate persons-attending, caught up in a mutual address. There are endless, and endlessly imaginative, interpretations of Job, but none is quite like this. Bugbee's poetic evocations let communion arise between the impersonality of things and our impersonality. He gives us an experiential grip on the text and its world. An academic or theological explication can no more replace this communion than hearing a performance of Beethoven can be replaced by studying the conductor's score. We're rapt in the finality of Job's Grandeurs, large and small.

A sense of being

His 1948 Berkeley dissertation, *The Sense and Conception of Being*, traces the aspiration for conceptual clarity and the aspiration for immediate, experiential access to reality through art, scripture, poetry, and music. He wants not just a *conception* of being but a *sense* of being peculiar to one's place. A *sense* of being appears in transforming moments of recognition, epiphany, or *Augenblick*. Consider this, from his PhD dissertation:

> [With the snow] each thing which had stood out, crying in resistance to the wind, now lapses and is lost in a pervasive still. Bird, bush,

mountain, animal, stick, and stone—each is left to itself, alone, as in timeless slumber. The wildness is sealed in silence … What blanches things visible, blotting mass and form, absorbing their very thinghood? What in this obscuring is hushedly revealing? What but the pure and secret presence that is snow?

The Inward Morning delivers wilderness, art, philosophy, and responsive receptivity in journal explorations. Shakespeare and Melville, as well as Plato, Eckhart, and Spinoza, make cameo appearances. The impressive reach of Bugbee's reading is reminiscent of Stanley Cavell, who held a fellowship at Harvard during Bugbee's time there. Cavell's readings of King Lear, Thoreau, Emerson, film, and opera are indicative of a transcendence of disciplinary specialization he shares with Bugbee.

We're reminded of Thoreau as we find Bugbee recalling childhood encounters with swamps, treks in the Canadian Rockies, and fishing the rivers of Northern California. His sense of wildness includes rowing in eights on the Schuylkill during his Princeton years and facing kamikaze fire on board the minesweeper he captained in the Pacific during the Second World War. And we can't help but notice echoes of Biblical wilderness: "Then Jesus was led by the Spirit into the wilderness" (Matthew 4:1–11); and "They encamped in the wilderness" (Exodus 19:2).

Bugbee's wilderness reflections climax in the entry for Friday, August 7, 1953. Here he puzzles over the powers of wilderness to awaken him. The passage leans forward to his essay on *Job*, and backward to his *Dissertation* passages on snow.

What this all meant, I could not say, kept trying to say, kept trying to harmonize with the suggestions arising from the things I read. But I do remember that this walking in the presence of things came to a definitive stage. It was in the fall of '41, October and November, while late autumn prevailed throughout the northern Canadian Rockies, restoring everything in that vast region to a native wildness. Some part of each day or night, for forty days, flurries of snow were flying. I weighed everything by the measure of the silent presence of things, clarified in the racing clouds, clarified by the cry of hawks, solidified in the presence of rocks, spelled syllable by syllable by waters of manifold voice, and consolidated in the act of taking steps, each step a meditation steeped in reality. The aspens and larches took on a yellow so vivid, so pure and trembling in the air, as to fairly cry out that they were as they were, limitlessly. And it was there in attending to this wildness, with unremitting alertness and attentiveness, yes, even as I slept, that I knew myself to have been instructed for life, though I was at a loss to say what instruction I had received.[9]

Here are roiling, rolling meanings lost and present. Here is a stammering attempt to convey this informing disquiet. These are thoughts taken up ten years later in "A Way of Reading Job." We are immersed in stillness, in experiential clarity and cognitive opacity. We are immersed in steadiness among bountiful things of creation: clouds, hawks, rocks, waters, snow. There is a Biblical motif here. Forty days in the Rockies recapitulates Jesus's forty-day wilderness fast. Each retreat preludes new life.

The Whirlwind delivers things-happening in a majestic musical voice. Bugbee delivers things-happening musically: flurries fly; things are clarified in clouds, by the cry of hawks, in the presence of rocks. The lines beg to be read aloud as music—as poetry, lyrical Psalms. "S" sibilants are repeated, hissing like water over the hard*ness* of rock*s* or the crying of hawk*s*. There are aspen*s* and larche*s*, and things "*s*olidified in the pre*s*ence of rock*s*, *s*pelled *s*yllable by *s*yllable by water*s* of manifold voi*ce*." The softly sustained "s" will sooth as it flows.

These walking meditations remind us of cloister walks, or wanderings in Galilee, or Thoreau's pilgrimage in "Walking." The powerful-yet-quiet attention to place reappears, as we've seen, in Bugbee's meditation on Job. Here in *The*

Inward Morning his wilderness walk yields an epiphany: he knows himself "to have been instructed for life—though [he is] at a loss to say what instruction [he] had received."[10]

This is a signal admission from a seasoned philosopher. What is an instruction that can't be told? But it is precisely his unassuming yet profound admission of ignorance that keeps us listening. We can hazard a response he hesitates to utter. He's caught between knowledge and revelation, between provincial wisdom and sublime Spirit. He has no proposition, adage, or simple counsel to print out. Nevertheless, his definitive appreciation is counsel, teaching. The instruction received is to be receptive to the cry of hawks and presence of rocks; to hear the lesson of aspens and larches that "fairly cry out that they [are] as they [are], limitlessly." He has been instructed to yield to the voices of beings of heaven-and-earth.

The lesson of forty days in the Rockies is the lesson of Isaiah 55:12:

> You will go out in joy, and be led forth in peace;
> the mountains and hills will burst into song before you,
> and all the trees of the field will clap their hands.[11]

For Bugbee, philosophy is "an approximation to a poem," wed to the local and individual—a walking meditation that is ineluctably first person. Consider Kelly Dean Jolley:

> Philosophical problems incarnate are now my meditation. Philosophical problems disincarnate no longer exert much pull on me. Perhaps what I have come to appreciate more fully is that there is a strict specificity about philosophical problems—they exist only in a specific person and they can be grappled with only in conjunction with that person and they can be solved—in whatever sense they are solved—only by that person. Philosophical problems arise from and are only finally responsive to the living experience of a specific person.[12]

This denies the detached "reportorial" or "spectator's" third-person stance toward the world and others, so characteristic of British empiricism, logical positivism, and a good deal of Anglophone philosophy. A disincarnate speaking to all-and-nobody derails the quest for personal meaning that should be the calling of philosophy and, in a wider sense, the calling of a mortal human life.

Henry Bugbee's being instructed by snow and still-standing trees is spirit incarnate among things of the world. His is a walking beholding *in whom* incarnate spirit is addressed by things that *themselves* incarnate spirit. Each is bound to the other in discrete address. It's not just *humans* who speak. Trees speak and bespeak. Thus, philosophy's musings and reflections come to resemble "a walking meditation of the place." This is a prayer-like receptivity infinitely responsive to the tissues and fissures of our being in the world.

5
Melville: What philosophers learn at sea

All men live enveloped in whale-line, are born with halters round their necks; And if you be a philosopher, though seated in the whale-boat, you would not at heart feel one whit more of terror, than though seated before your evening fire with a poker, and not a harpoon, by your side.

***

Where lies the final harbor, whence we unmoor no more? I still bathe me in eternal mildness of joy.

—*Moby-Dick*

The broad plot of *Moby-Dick* needs no retelling. What's fascinating is how Melville can so seamlessly and happily clasp a sort of philosophy to literature and religion—and both to occasionally demonic theology. I link what I'll call an informal, conversational, and episodic philosophy to a renegade theology and both to the literary forms of this novel. The reward is a tumult of philosophical, theological, and literary energy.

Seas of unknowing

The novel presents multiple perspectives on life, and multiple actual forms of life, each lodged in intense and immense surrounds. This is not formal philosophy driving toward lucid conclusions. Its endless advance and retreat disappoint all hope for a composite picture or conclusion. This is informal philosophy, embedded in life and death. It doesn't resolve what Melville sees as the eternal enigmas of human existence but displays them. We sail in misty, dangerous, sometimes happy, ever-unfolding waters.

The meaning of the white whale or divinity, of love and comradery, of demonic powers of hatred, are elusive. Melville, Ishmael, and others seek flashes of insight. "[T]hrough all the thick mists of the dim doubts in my mind, divine intuitions now and then shoot, enkindling my fog with a heavenly ray."[1] We await "divine intuition." No climax of conviction about the sense of it arrives.

Formal philosophy aims for answers, even the despairing answer that there are none. Literature dispenses with this expectation of closure. It imagines endless situations and apparent resolutions, feeling no necessity to promise or deliver definitive results. This indeterminacy can exhilarate—as if the world were richer for harboring not just the known but the unknown. We needn't succumb to the fate of Narcissus:

> because he could not grasp the … image he saw in the fountain, [he] plunged into it and was drowned. But that same image, we ourselves see in all rivers and oceans: the image of the ungraspable phantom of life; and this is the key to it all.[2]

We can find our face in shifting waters without falling in. Wonder supervenes on unknowing:

> [W]e now gazed at the most wondrous phenomenon which the secret seas have hitherto revealed to mankind. A vast pulpy mass lay floating on the water, innumerable long arms radiating from its centre as if blindly to clutch at any hapless object within reach. No perceptible face or front did it have but undulated there on the billows, an unearthly, formless, chance-like apparition of life.[3]

Formless like the fog or the sea, this is the giant squid.

Whales

The whale is unknown. While alive its bulk lies under its skin; it swims in the depths mainly unseen. The unknown whale, Moby Dick, shape-shifts toward an angry Old Testament God or a watery Demon. It elicits fearful reverence in Starbuck, and in others of the crew:

> It cannot be much matter of surprise that some whalemen should [declare] Moby Dick not only ubiquitous, but immortal; should [he] ever be made to spout thick blood, such a sight would be but a ghastly deception; in … billows hundreds of leagues away, his unsullied jet would once more be seen.[4]

Christ resurfaces after death. The whale will resurface—no matter if killed. This is the crew's piety. In contrast, Ahab is hatefully heretical:

> That inscrutable thing is chiefly what I hate. Be the white whale agent [of another Power] or be the white whale [the] principal [Power, God], I will wreak … hate upon him. Talk not to me of blasphemy, man; I'd strike the sun if it insulted me.[5]

Whale and God challenge Ahab, who mocks Divine omniscience: God can't be all-knowing, for he knows not his own genesis. Kant says we can't know what's behind appearances. This induces humility. Ahab won't be so denied and humbled:

> The sweet tinges of sunset skies and woods; yea, and the gilded velvets of butterflies, and the butterfly cheeks of young girls; all these are but subtile deceits, not actually inherent in substances, but only laid on from without; so that all deified Nature absolutely paints like the harlot, whose allurements cover nothing but the charnel-house within.[6]

Nature is hateful, her beautiful appearance, a trick: the "butterfly cheeks of young girls" hide a harlot's painted face. Nature is whore-some.

Schopenhauer puts the wonder of music at the inner core of things; Ahab finds repulsive stench. Our narrator, Ishmael, gives an alternative to Ahab's hate and disgust. With regard to his genesis, he embodies a placid unconcern: his birthplace, family, and youth are unknown. His biblical namesake is cast into wilderness. Ishmael wanders the wilderness of the seas, an innocent first son in exile.

Bulkington embodies mysterious unknowability, too, arriving god-like from a shadowy nowhere. He's beautiful, charismatic—and vanishes.

Take heart, take heart, O Bulkington! Bear thee grimly, demigod! Up from the spray of thy ocean-perishing—straight up, leaps thy apotheosis![7]

His charisma might have offset Ahab's—had he lived.

Socratic unknowing

In pursuing the meaning of the whale, Ahab's demonic obsession, or Pip's strange access to Ahab's heart, we get versions of Socratic *devotion* to truth while being denied the satisfactions of attaining it. Socrates knows only that he doesn't know. He casts his companions and readers into unknowing. Yet this is not skepticism, nor is Melville a skeptic, despite denying us stable truth.

For Socrates the resolutions I seek won't come from him. Only I, in the particularity of my insights and passions, can provide resolutions. They will be personal resolutions, holding not eternally but episodically. Socrates and Melville reveal plural truths that beckon episodically without eternal warrant. Truths come to individual inquirers, one by one, and will be partial and context-bound. There are no rousing, cymbal-clashing truths to proclaim from the summit.

This unfinished dogma-free path deposits us always on the cusp of new experience. Philosophy here begins and ends in wonder. I call it "living philosophy," a personal love of wisdom responsive to the issue of the moment as persons tread uncertain paths. The face of philosophy becomes as mobile and shifting as the changing vistas of the sea.

D. M. McKinnon captures the inevitability of episodic philosophy:

> One cannot by magic escape the conditions of humanity, assume the absolute perspective of God. If it is better to arrive than to travel, we are still inescapably travelling ... And our perspectives are necessarily those of travelers, at least for most of the time. But there still remains a difference between the traveler who takes the measure of his road and the one who seeks to be oblivious of its windings.[8]

For Melville, glimpses of truth appear in lively or melancholy gestures, moods, exchanges, and meditations among the exotic crew. Pip's glimpse is not Starbuck's; Queequeg's is not Ishmael's; Flask's is not Ahab's. Each has a moment in the unfolding tapestry. Each looks on others (who look back) creating shifting ensembles. There are multiple truths to be existentially weighed. These are truths from the trenches.[9]

Ishmael is a somewhat unifying force. He earns a presumptive reliability, a perspective on bourgeoning accumulations of perspectives. He is a steady, unflinching storyteller who lives to tell the tale. He cites *Job*: "And I only am escaped alone to tell thee."[10] And we're invited to repeat the journey. If we join up again, the telling will start again from the top, replicating life's eternal repetitions.

The very idea of an unfinished, episodic philosophy, allied with literature and rumors of religion, is dismissed by most post-medieval philosophy. Since Descartes, philosophy aspires to formality and impersonality. The varieties and textures of felt-realities are filtered out as flimsy. Philosophy takes its lead from math and science. Thoreau, Nietzsche, and Melville dissent. They seek episodic, particular "difficult realities" where discrete individuals prosper or fail, find eloquence or boredom, move forward or backward or just trudge in place.

Modern philosophical tradition aims at a purity and precision that all rational minds must accept, full of airtight arguments and universal principles. They eschew the tangled bogs and heavens of Melville's living and dying souls. Plato's sketch of a city-state aims for rational purity and order (at least on first reading), as does Kant's deduction of the categories or Spinoza's demonstrations. But there's a counter-movement: the passionate and partial poetic philosophies of Nietzsche or Emerson, Montaigne or Kierkegaard, Wittgenstein or Cavell.[11] They decline abstract scientific impersonality; they give us existential bite.

We worry that if subjectivity—respect for messy, difficult felt-realities—is given a foothold, then the hard-earned prestige of scientific objectivity will be compromised. But we can have multifold vision. Melville gives an objective account of whale-zoology and a subjective account of the whale's magnificence. Poetic philosophies welcome the varieties of lived experience. An impressionistic subjectivity is no more subversive of science than Bach and Erasmus are subversive of biology. We treasure the felt-realities of friends and lovers, children and neighbors, gardens and landscapes, music and sport. And also treasure discoveries in astronomy.[12]

The lilt of selves immersed in life's flow is the "metaphysical riot" that Cavell finds in Melville, Hawthorne, Emerson, Thoreau, and Dickinson. They put souls at risk and take metaphysics seriously.[13] In Melville, powerful, lyrical reflections arise impromptu from the unschooled mouths of memorable characters. Queequeg, the "cannibal," works dangerously on the slippery back of a dead whale tied precariously to the ship. Ishmael tethers him from a spar high above and muses on the rope that binds them:

> for better or for worse, we two, for the time, were wedded; and should poor Queequeg sink to rise no more, then both usage and honor demanded, that instead of cutting the cord, it should drag me down in his wake.[14]

Ishmael proposes that personal obligation erases free will:

So strongly and metaphysically did I conceive of my situation then, that while earnestly watching his motions, I seemed distinctly to perceive that my own individuality was now merged in a joint stock company of two; that my free will had received a mortal wound; and that another's mistake or misfortune might plunge innocent me into unmerited disaster and death.[15]

Reflections arrive solo, in chatting among shipmates, and in intense dialogue. We'll hear the vivid exchange between Ahab and Pip patterned on King Lear and his fool. And nature herself can be addressed. Here is Ahab:

Then hail, forever hail, O sea, in whose eternal tossings the wild fowl finds his only rest. Born of earth, yet suckled by the sea; though hill and valley mothered me, ye billows are my foster-brothers![16]

Though its reality is fleeting, for the moment he inhabits a mothering, abundant reality.

Intimate abundance

Melville can soar into mystic realms, but he's not a Platonist. He's too disorderly for that and too disorderly to be Aristotelian. If you don't mind hyphenated identities, he's a Romantic-Vitalist—earth, sea, and stars are alive. Galileo inaugurates a materialism of sticks, stones, and atoms. Melville's natural world bespeaks wonder, life, death, and struggle. It bursts with this-worldly poetic-religious light and dark.[17] It owes nothing to Platonic or Christian orbs:

The industrious earth beneath was as a weaver's loom, with a gorgeous carpet on it, whereof the ground-vine tendrils formed the warp and woof, and the living flowers the figures.[18]

And it is not always innocent:

Under an abated sun; afloat all day upon smooth, slow heaving swells; Seated in his boat, light as a birch canoe; and so sociably mixing with the soft waves themselves ... these are the times of dreamy quietude, when beholding the tranquil beauty and brilliancy of the ocean's skin, one forgets the tiger heart that pants beneath it; and would not willingly remember, that this velvet paw but conceals a remorseless fang.[19]

Even as waves become sociable, and swells become cradling, velvet paws hide remorseless fangs. The Good and Beautiful are abundant, immanent, and vie with The Terrible and Devouring. Reverie and reality are co-articulate:

[There are] the mild blue hill-sides; as over these there steals the hush, the hum; you almost swear that play-wearied children lie sleeping in these solitudes ... And all this mixes with your most mystic mood; so that fact and fancy, half-way meeting, interpenetrate, and form one seamless whole.[20]

Playfully but seriously, Ishmael paints metaphysical spoutings:

I am convinced that from the heads of all ponderous profound beings, such as Plato, Pyrrho, the Devil, Jupiter, Dante, and so on, there always goes up a certain semi-visible steam, while in the act of thinking deep thoughts.[21]

Imaginings can be rooted in ideas but are more likely to be triggered by whales, thunderclaps, intoxicating moons, or the scent of sea creatures. This is the "mystic mood" of poetry, of befitting reverie, where fact and fancy meet.[22]

Drama

An episodic philosophy is fitted for high drama. Here is Queequeg, a confessed "cannibal," and the kindest companion and roommate. He practices Ramadan, sitting cross-legged through the night, keeping a rigorous fast.[23] On the way from New Bedford to Nantucket, after rescuing an overboard rube who had insulted him, he remarks "We cannibals must help these Christians."[24] Ishmael is a tolerant, cultural Christian:

> I cherish the greatest respect towards everybody's religious obligations, never mind how comical, and could not find it in my heart to undervalue even a congregation of ants worshipping a toad-stool.[25]

He begs Queequeg to give up Ramadan, but his bedroom harangue is good humored and intimate. Discussions among professors are never so cozy:

> "Queequeg," said I, "get into bed now, and lie and listen to me." I then went on, beginning with the rise and progress of the primitive religions, and coming down to the various religions of the present.[26]

If we abstract "the argument" to diagram for class we'd lose wit, affections, and Ishmael's generosity. Plato takes philosophy as care for the soul, and in this case it's the embodied soul. Ishmael tucks Queequeg in: night fasts are unhealthy.

Plato's *Symposium* starts with camaraderie: shared drink and dinner and ends with a flirtatious feud between lust and love. Ishmael's critique of Ramadan proceeds as he tucks in his friend. Reasons flow from care and affectionate play. Ishmael doesn't place Christian practice above Queequeg's "savage" or "Muslim" practice. Lent is as bad for the body as Ramadan. Thinking arrives with Eros and humor, in everyday gestures—sleeping, drinking, eating, pacing, rowing, climbing.

Speech can be wise, conventional, or foolish. Life's pauses and movements can bespeak things wise, conventional, or foolish. Bodily presence can bespeak metaphysical moods. Ahab's body-length scar and hobbling peg leg bespeak terror and doom:

Threading its way out from among his grey hairs, and continuing right down one side of his tawny scorched face and neck … you saw a slender rod-like mark, lividly whitish. It resembled that perpendicular seam sometimes made in the straight, lofty trunk of a great tree, when the upper lightning tearingly darts down it, and without wrenching a single twig, peels and grooves out the bark from top to bottom, ere running off into the soil.[27]

His scar and peg-legged pacing modulate his thought and speech. Equally, his speech modulates his pacing. Together they shape him.[28]

6

Where is God?: Ahab at sea

deep down and deep inland
there I still bathe me
in eternal mildness of joy.
—ISHMAEL

No one reads *Moby-Dick* consecutively, cover to cover—no breaks. Sometimes fans gather for a library reading, passing the baton on to a new voice every ten pages, for as many days as it takes. These are annual events in New Bedford, on Nantucket, and elsewhere.

Defiance

The infinite world is episodically realized in a ramble of pacing, laughing, listening, and speaking. We get little cosmos. Take Ahab's twisted stance toward "God"—a presumably stable religious-metaphysical posit. Ahab addresses a Thou and equally calls it *Fraud*. Passions undergird his wild unwisdom, the most dramatic of which is defiance.

> Thou knowest not how came ye, hence callest thyself unbegotten; certainly knowest not thy beginning, hence callest thyself unbegun. I know that of me, which thou knowest not of thyself, oh, thou omnipotent.[1]

Ignorant of His origins, this "God" must bow to Ahab's knowledge. Divinity's claims to eternity and creative power also get mocked:

> There is some unsuffusing thing beyond thee, thou clear spirit, to whom all thy eternity is but time, all thy creativeness [merely] mechanical. Through thee, thy flaming self, my scorched eyes do dimly see it.[2]

Ahab sees pretense in a "refiner's fire." This would-be omnipotence is orphaned, grieving, alone and beyond comfort:

> Oh, thou foundling fire, thou hermit immemorial, thou too hast thy incommunicable riddle, thy unparticipated [unshared] grief. Here again with haughty agony, I read my sire. Leap! leap up and lick the sky! I leap with thee; I burn with thee; would fain be welded with thee; defyingly I worship thee![3]

Can worship be *defiant* and *irreverent*? Ahab leaps heavenward with his godhead. "My sire" is ambiguous. God may have sired him, or *he* may have sired God! A leap to embrace this "blindfolded" divinity "welds" mortal to immortal:

> Oh, oh! Yet blindfold, yet will I talk to thee. Light though thou be, thou leapest out of darkness; but I am darkness leaping out of light, leaping out of thee![4]

"God" becomes light emerging from darkness. But light can't illuminate its own dark beginnings without a second source of light. Thus, the first light, God, is functionally orphaned, blind to its source.

This is mad. Ahab is primal darkness; God leaps from him. Only dark Power can say "let there be light!" Ahab can see both his own and God's origins. As Prince of Darkness, he leaps from the brow of this blind, foundling god.

On these seas I as Persian once did worship [thee], till in the sacramental act so burned by thee, that to this hour I bear the scar; I now know thee, thou clear spirit, and I now know that thy right worship is defiance. To neither love nor reverence wilt thou be kind; and e'en for hate thou canst but kill; and all are killed. No fear-less fool now fronts thee. I own [grant] thy speechless, placeless power; but to the last gasp of my earthquake life will dispute its unconditional, unintegral mastery in me. In the midst of the personified impersonal, a personality stands here.[5]

The attack on this demonic "speechless, placeless power" becomes Ahab's hate-filled welding to speechless Moby-Dick:

Towards thee I roll, thou all-destroying but unconquering whale; to the last I grapple with thee; from hell's heart I stab at thee; for hate's sake I spit my last breath at thee.[6]

The whale may destroy him but can't conquer his spitting defiance. Moby-Dick is tangible magnificence and power, while God is illusory magnificence and power—a miserable foundling to stab at. Ahab takes vengeance on any beast or divinity who would refuse his Magnificence. He welds himself to his harpoon and to the whale he would kill. He "would fain be welded" to his God—and would kill Him.[7]

Yet even his vengeance is fickle. Ahab is suffused in compassion, as he asks to be tenderly riveted to the slightly crazed cabin boy, Pip—a foundling, a holy fool. This is the Shakespearean moment when Lear seeks instruction from his fool. Ahab basks in a tender moment not unlike Ishmael's:

Amid the tornadoed Atlantic of my being, do I myself still for ever centrally disport in mute calm; and while ponderous planets of unwaning woe revolve round me, deep down and deep inland there I still bathe me in eternal mildness of joy.[8]

In scenes like these, tremendous energy overflows in dissonances of mortals and immortals, sense and nonsense, hatred and joy, bereavement and repair:

> Shall I call that wise or foolish; if it be really wise it has a foolish look to it; yet, if it be foolish, then has it a sort of wise-ish look to it.[9]

Genre

Melville writes what's called a novel, and some think it's an adventure tale. But we have a haphazard collection: short dramatic pieces with characters given lines, as if we were opening the pages of a script; long disquisitions on biology or cetology; near-Biblical musings; extended monologue, and so forth.

In *Hamlet*, Polonius presents

> the best actors in the world, either for tragedy, comedy, history, pastoral, pastoral-comical, historical-comical, tragical-comical-historical, one-act plays or long poems.[10]

Melville delivers long meditations, dramas (each player named), rollicking adventures, biology, extended overtures, and finales.

The prologue to the novel provides an assembly of words for "whale" from dozens of languages. A "sub-sub-librarian" assembles a catalogue of passages citing whales. If this sub-librarian were to confront *Moby-Dick*, he'd try to nail down the genre—but without success. It's "historical-comical, tragical-comical-historical, full of one-act plays or a long and unlimited poem." A good reader will leave sub-sub-librarians aside to dive with Ishmael into wildness. Moods and perspectives shift and conflict. Genre escapes us. Yet there is a subtle progress of scenarios: wonder and terror at creation's abundance; unfolding tales of catastrophe; bursts of new life, as in *The Book of Job*'s majestic Creator-Whirlwind, impressed by its own wildness, and the infinite ingenuity of its scope.[11]

Moby-Dick is not just about destructions or a vengeful God, or a vengeful sea-captain, or a place of slaughter:

> another and still stranger world met our eyes as we gazed over the side. For, suspended in those watery vaults, floated the forms of the nursing mothers of the whales … and as human infants while suckling will calmly and fixedly gaze away from the breast, as if leading two different lives at the time; and while yet drawing mortal nourishment, be still spiritually feasting upon some unearthly reminiscence;—even so, did the young of these whales seem looking up towards us, but not at us, as if we were but a bit of Gulf-weed in their new-born sight.[12] Sucklings are without hate and soulful—eyes raised toward heaven.

This tender serenity is redemptive. The emerging scenario is divine and comedic. Killers set harpoons to rest. Awe and affection and serenity hover. There is a pulse of affirmation and rebirth. Death and disaster retreat.[13]

Rebirth and renewal

"Call me Ishmael." Is this his birth name? Perhaps it's the *nom de plume* of an otherwise anonymous storyteller, anticipating new life in the wilds. Perhaps he's born with his story of adventure, disaster, and rebirth, as the biblical Ishmael is reborn as he survives wilderness. The writer who says "Call me Ishmael" is cast out of a tribe of schoolteachers and pupils to be reborn at sea, author of his own story. A wonder of emerging from nowhere is matched by a wonder of surviving disaster, and then a wonder of a tale brought to birth. Only he lives to tell. As Job survives his afflictions and the Whirlwind, Ishmael survives the whirlpool that swallows the Pequod.

In *Genesis*, God delivers light from waste and welter, "tohu-wabohu," a place without form and void.[14] Melville's *Genesis* is from the darkness of

Ishmael's emergence to his birth on the sea, from disaster at sea to a rebirth of teller and tale. Ishmael drifts suicidally in darkness through the streets of Manhattan. Leaving the wasteland of the city, shipboard order ensues. Waste and welter return in the whale chase and final disaster. Then birth once more as the story survives to be told. If order never arrives for good, neither does Death gain full dominion. Genesis concludes with the image of a mummy in a coffin.[15] Queequeg makes himself a coffin that becomes the life buoy Ishmael clasps in the vortex devouring the ship. He survives to tell tales of deaths and rebirths.

Tashtego works on the whale laid out on the deck. He squeezes into the head's narrow spout hole, working down to retrieve valuable ambergris. The carcass slips suddenly to the sea. Trapped, Tashtego plunges doom-ward. Queequeg dives in, pulling him from the birth canal. In a comic touch, he turns Tashtego's leg to avoid breech birth from the spout hole:

> Upon first thrusting in for him, a leg was presented; but well knowing that that was not as it ought to be, and might occasion great trouble;—he had thrust back the leg, and by a dexterous heave and toss, had wrought a somerset upon the Indian; so that with the next trial, he came forth in the good old way—head foremost.[16]

Queequeg is midwife at Tashtego's rebirth.[17]

Deaths and rebirths

It ends with the rebirth of the teller of sea tales. It begins with satirical prefaces laying out purgatory: the hunt for whale names and whale quotes rather than whales. It features death and disaster, bookish mediocrity, and heroic action. We laugh at the sub-sub-librarian, but the laugh is on scholars who bicker over genres: is this "tragedy, comedy, history, pastoral—hyperbolic truth, true hyperbole, sublime lie—epic, novel, poem, mash-up"? One lesson of *Moby-Dick* is the plea to flail in wilds rather than argue over labels.

> There is no staying in any one place; for at one and the same time everything has to be done everywhere. It is much the same with him who endeavors the descriptions of the scene.[18]

Flux and instability are pervasive. Even the epilogue is unstable: "Only I have survived to tell ye." The citation is from *Job* and gives Ishmael gravitas. Yet it also inserts doubt. Why believe a wild story not a soul can confirm? Why believe in biblical tales or in Melville's fictions? "I only am escaped alone to tell thee … The drama's done. Why then here does anyone step forth?—Because one did survive the wreck."[19] We believe—or don't.

The book, the sea, the ship, the whale, the crew—each is an exhausting infinity. We need a break to collect ourselves. Then inch ahead.

Color, sanity, truths

Melville embraces racial and religious diversity without preaching. He shows virtue in a fraternal community where race and cultural differences drop away. He appoints Ishmael to narrate, and the "cannibal" to be his best friend. Queequeg's religion is a hodgepodge of rituals. He observes Ramadan by night (rather than day) and is puritanically circumspect about exposing private parts: not genitals, but feet. He crawls under the bed rather than be exposed changing socks. He is more selflessly Christian than the would-be Christians who taunt him on the ferry to Nantucket. He dives in to save one who's fallen overboard.

We're immersed in joy and sadness, kindness and cruelty, melancholy and exuberance. And amidst madness we have sanity. Nothing can replace immersion in the power of Melville's lines and paragraphs. Enter the vengeful Ahab approaching the half-drowned, half-mad Pip, with uncommon tenderness. It's Shakespearean:

Ahab whispers: —Thou touchest my inmost centre, boy; thou art tied to me by cords woven of my heart-strings. Come, let's down.

Pip asks: —What's this? here's velvet shark-skin. He intently gazes at Ahab's hand. Is it velvet or shark, mad or sane? Both!

Pip continues: —Ah, now, had poor Pip but felt so kind a thing as this, perhaps he had ne'er been lost! This seems to me, sir, as a man-rope; something that weak souls may hold by.

Pip pleads: —Oh, sir, let old Perth now come and rivet these two hands together; the black one with the white, for I will not let this go.

Ahab responds: —Oh, boy, nor will I thee, unless I should thereby drag thee to worse horrors than are here. Come, then, to my cabin.

Ahab continues, bitter yet tender: —Lo! ye believers in gods all goodness, and in man all ill, lo you! see the omniscient gods oblivious of suffering man; and man, though idiotic, and knowing not what he does, yet full of the sweet things of love and gratitude. Come! I feel prouder leading thee by thy black hand, than though I grasped an Emperor's![20]

In pre-Civil War America, by Southern lights, these last words are disgusting and seditious, and by many Northern lights, they are heroically humane. The scene taps justice and compassion through and through.

A line of simple wisdom follows from the chorus, played by the Manxman. The old Manxman mutters:

—There go two daft ones now. One daft with strength, the other daft with weakness. [21]

Partial views

Elsewhere enter the Captain, Starbuck, and Stubb on a clear day looking into the sea for an image of life. Each recounts what he sees—Ahab, moments of bliss amidst dark; Starbuck, love's deep joy; Stubb, invitations to dive and play. Here is Ahab, meadows replacing seas:

> Oh, grassy glades! oh, ever vernal endless landscapes in the soul; in ye, — though long parched by the dead drought of the earthy life, —in ye, men yet may roll, like young horses in new morning clover; and for some few fleeting moments, feel the cool dew of the life immortal on them. Would to God these blessed calms would last. But the mingled, mingling threads of life are woven by warp and woof: calms crossed by storms, a storm for every calm.[22]

He wonders plaintively where it will end:

> Where lies the final harbor, whence we unmoor no more? In what rapt ether sails the world, of which the weariest will never weary? Where is the foundling's father hidden? Our souls are like those orphans whose unwedded mothers die in bearing them: the secret of our paternity lies in their grave, and we must there to learn it.[23]

And Ahab exposes utter and eloquent despair:

> Oh! time was, when as the sunrise nobly spurred me, so the sunset soothed. No more ... Gifted with the high perception, I lack the low, enjoying power; damned, most subtly and most malignantly! Damned in the midst of Paradise![24]

Strangely, Ahab's unbelief is now chastened:

> Oh, lonely death on lonely life! Oh, now I feel my topmost greatness lies in my topmost grief. Ho, ho! from all your furthest bounds, pour ye now in, ye bold billows of my whole foregone life ... let me then tow to pieces. [25]

Starbuck also seeks truth in the mirror of the sea, and finds pure beauty:

> And that same day, too, gazing far down from his boat's side into that same golden sea, Starbuck lowly murmured: "Loveliness unfathomable, as ever lover saw in his young bride's eye!—Tell me not of thy teeth-tiered sharks, and thy kidnapping cannibal ways. Let faith oust fact; let fancy oust memory; I look deep down and do believe."[26]

Now shift to the light-hearted Stubb:

> Stubb, fish-like, with sparkling scales, leaped up in that same golden light: —I am Stubb, and Stubb has his history; but here Stubb takes oaths that he has always been jolly![27]

There's no substitute for encountering these majestic evocations firsthand. We have truths rather than truth. But what holds these sea-gazers in community?

If Stubb, Starbuck, and Ahab have three different images of the sea, can it be the *same* sea they take in? *Yes, and no.* It's like seeing a building, first from the street, then from the sky, then from within. The limits of communication are the limits of shared perceptions. We have multiple viewing stations.

Melville multiplies angles of perception and withholds an absolute vantage point for comparison and ranking. I can never see a building's insides the way plumbers will; I'll be blind to nuance that's obvious to them. And the view from the attic is not the view from the basement. In a crude sense, all viewers see "the same sea" or the same building. Yet once perception becomes nuanced, characters do not scan the same sea—nor do the plumber and I see the same building.

It takes skill and goodwill to communicate across differences. My plumber may not be adept in presenting his angle to me. Starbuck may not be adept in conveying his view to Stubb or to Ahab. There may be nods of appreciation— or stares of incomprehension—as each tries to convey a take on the waters.

There is no rule book for communicating across aesthetic, moral, or religious differences. Even with careful listening and imagination, we will sometimes part ways disconnected.

Stubb, a fish who is jolly, won't understand Ahab, a demon. Ishmael understands both Ahab and Stubb, and Starbuck has capacious understanding. The Manxman understands neither Pip nor Ahab. It's futile to look for a single rock-bottom truth here. We understand each other, when we do, one by one, in passing. Too often we discover we've been wrong. Life goes on.

The communicative arena is not just bleak with despair. There are moments of heart-stopping awe. Men divergent in bearing and belief can congeal in awe and wonder:

> Suddenly the waters around them slowly swelled in broad circles; then quickly upheaved, as if sideways sliding from a submerged berg of ice, swiftly rising to the surface ... Shrouded in a thin drooping veil of mist, it hovered for a moment in the rainbowed air; and then fell swamping back into the deep. Crushed thirty feet upwards, the waters flashed for an instant like heaps of fountains, then brokenly sank in a shower of flakes, leaving the circling surface creamed like new milk round the marble trunk of the whale.[28]

Here, startling majesty, even a whiff of tenderness, transcends differences.

Always birth after death?

The magnificent story is one of birth, death, and rebirth—of death-lines tangled with birth-lines:

> Starbuck saw long coils of the umbilical cord of Madame Leviathan, by which the young cub seemed still tethered to its dam. [Often] this natural

line, with the maternal end loose, becomes entangled with the hempen one, so that the cub is thereby trapped. Some of the subtlest secrets of the seas seemed divulged to us in this enchanted pond.[29]

The tangled cords release life—and insure death. We're trapped betwixt and between. The last word might be a breakdown of life. The hunt brings death—or is it a breakthrough of life from disaster. Does it end with a sinking vessel—or a man saved by a coffin?

The story rolls on through disasters and rescues. We hope for life's joys: children, travel, health, gardens, music—so much more. Yet all life sinks toward death and is strewn with disaster. Realities are varied. The crew will die, their story doesn't. Immortality in—and of—story is the best immortality we'll get.

The desire to sum up life in a ledger of joys and abjections is as futile as the desire to understand things-in-themselves apart from their appearances. It's no good to freeze life—even if we could—to tally wins and losses. The Pequod is destroyed. The whale hunt destroys. Which is the greater? A "cunning brute" hunts down another "cunning brute." There's no weighing one hunt, one brutishness, against others. And destructions are mixed with triumphs of friendship, bravery, and compassion. We discard all ledgers.

A hemp line brings a whale to death, while the coils of an umbilical cord bespeak life. We're caught in the life and death of whales, men, mothers, demigods, tyrants, holy fools. All but Ishmael are brought to the bottom. He clings to Queequeg's coffin and is reborn to tell of devastations, madness, brides in the sea, tenderness in mothering whales:

> [W]e were now in that enchanted calm which they say lurks at the heart of every commotion. And still in the distracted distance we beheld … successive pods of whales, eight or ten in each, swiftly going round and round, like multiplied spans of horses in a ring … We must watch for a breach in the living wall that hemmed us in; the wall that had only admitted us in order to shut us up.[30]

Within the vortex we find "Madame Leviathan," nursing, moving in regenerative curves. This reverses the swirl that swallows the Pequod:

> First, the whales forming the margin of our lake began to crowd a little, and tumble against each other, as if lifted by half spent billows from afar; then the lake itself began faintly to heave and swell; the submarine bridal-chambers and nurseries vanished.[31]

The best of times, though priceless, may be short-lived. In any case, sinking ships are not the last or only word:

> And thus, though surrounded by circle upon circle of consternations and affrights, did these inscrutable creatures at the centre freely and fearlessly indulge in all peaceful concernments; yea, serenely reveled in dalliance and delight. But even so do I myself disport in mute calm; and while ponderous planets of unwaning woe revolve round me, deep down and deep inland there I still bathe me in eternal mildness of joy.[32]

These words are not easily reconciled with a Melville remembered for melancholy, rage, or for a pernicious whale hunt deservedly crushed. Yet Ishmael declares, "I myself ... still bathe me in eternal mildness of joy."[33] He sits in astonished quiet:

> As I sat there at my ease, cross-legged on the deck; after the bitter exertion at the windlass; under a blue tranquil sky; the ship under indolent sail, and gliding so serenely along ... I felt divinely free from all ill-will, or petulance, or malice, of any sort whatsoever.[34]

In "eternal mildness of joy" he survives, bespeaking a strange resurrection, and in his grand multi-chaptered memorial to the dead, bequeaths them a kind of immortality.[35]

7

Intimate communions

Philosophers in nineteenth-century Europe—Feuerbach, Hegel, Kierkegaard, Marx, Nietzsche—were obsessed with the range and legitimacy of religion. Hegel, the leading thinker of the time, framed religion as a social-historical construct. Kierkegaard disagreed. To be Christian is not to be a loyal church member, nor someone ceremonially baptized. At most, this might constitute a "file identity" of interest to bureaucracies but without personal heft.

To be Christian in Kierkegaard's view is a matter of the heart, of a sensibility that is dynamic and multifaceted. Within a Christian sensibility you relate self-reflectively to others, and to the unfurling lilt and tang of life. You flourish in the intimate communions of grief, love, and celebration, of singing and reciting, of aesthetic and moral insight, of feasting and fasting. This sensibility is both personal and interpersonal, a "dense concoction of imperatives, yearnings, reflections, actions, joys, tragedies, laughter, and tears."[1] Let's look at Kierkegaard's brilliant early text, *Fear and Trembling*, where communions, intimacies, and religious sensibilities come into play.

As we know too well, Abraham is ordered to sacrifice his son. Kierkegaard's "Dialectical Lyric" poetically evokes Abraham's plight. Sensibility—in this case, Abraham's—is not a set of rules to obey or disobey but a tilt of the heart, best conveyed poetically. Johannes de silentio, gives multiple evocations of the patriarch's response to the order to sacrifice. None satisfies him.[2] Yet quite apart from understanding Abraham's faith, these evocations throw light on communion, religious sensibility, and intimate life.

The rights and wrongs of child sacrifice or of obedience to God remain undiscussed and murky. Nevertheless, we get a visceral sense of modes of intimate attachment and separation in personal life. Principles—say, unstinting obedience to God, or the primacy of religion over ethics, or the primacy of ethical love for sons over divine calls to kill—are suspended.[3] Yet sensibilities of faith, communion, and intimacy are vividly present and evolving.

Fear and Trembling meanders in *search* of faith, starting with four different Abrahams climbing Moriah. Kierkegaard pairs each Abraham portrait with a short meditation on a mother weaning her infant. Intimacy and communion are put through trials. Everyday weaning is cast as a test that parallels Abraham's. Is Abraham weaning Isaac? Is God weaning Abraham? Weaning is intimacy-and-communion—and faith under a greater or lesser stress.

Sensibility is a child of imagination and heart. Beyond four Abrahams and mothers, Johannes gives us another surprisingly simple image of faith. He sketches a cheerful burgher trudging faithfully home from work. The burgher thinks of his wife and the lamb she has prepared for dinner. If the lamb is not there? Is this a loss or crisis? Faith triumphs over despair as the burgher happily trudges home. This is a purely comic test of faith. Sensibility also appears in a romantic tale of near-faith. Johannes gives us a young man suffering love lost. Does he have faith his love will be returned? He does not, and so he's a person who falls short of faith. In yet another sketch, Johannes gives us Socrates seeking intimate wisdom—as if his embrace of ignorance were a kind of faith. Will he be granted wisdom, as the Burgher hopes for lamb, and Abraham hopes for Isaac's return? We are teased with questions-without-answers. Yet throughout, faith keeps company with trials of communion and intimacy.

Intimacy and subjectivity

Intimacy, heartfeltness, and mutuality among persons are central to faith. The slogan "Truth is subjectivity" means that a truth we can live and die for inheres in the animated lives of subjects rather than any static domain of objects or "brute facts." When it comes to science, news reporting, historical research, and factual exchange, truth calls for objectivity. But objectivity and subjectivity are often coordinated in practice: think of a compassionate doctor delivering objective medical news. Subjective objectivity is not always an oxymoron.

A religious sensibility—surely a subjective matter—may have a face turned toward a state of affairs. I feel passionate about the starry heavens above. Yet a religious sensibility is not founded on objective truths about the world—say truths about starry heavens. Nor is sensibility founded on creeds taken to express objective truths. Nor can this sensibility be reduced to objectively specifiable social practices like church attendance. Religious sensibility resembles poetic or musical sensibility.

Although it may be hard to get *total* agreement, in many cases we can identify who has such a sensibility and who doesn't, whether it's musical or religious. And a religious or musical sensibility is not primarily solitary. A poet requires other poets to learn from and sing to and with. Musicians require other musicians for tips on style and technique, if nothing else. Persons of faith find their subjective religious sensibilities in dialogue—in prayers and singing with others. A sensibility includes personal responsiveness, shared passions, testimony, and avowals. Mine interweaves with yours in heartfelt projects and witness. Even nature can greet us subjectively: waves sing, and night mists speak, intimately.

Modern bureaucratic-market cultures are engorged with omnivorous, impersonal objectivity. We become a set of file numbers, passwords, and bank accounts, not to mention our gender, consumer, and ethnic identities.

Kierkegaard scorns the tendency to objectify the question whether one is Christian. One's faith can't be reduced to baptism records or to recorded attestations of belief.[4] A moment of religious sensibility—say an intimate extension of love or mercy—is dynamic. It is not a static belief, doctrine, or social status.

As Kierkegaard views it, public proclamations by state-paid Bishops are irreligious. Faith is found in the intimacy of my heartfelt avowals as they intersect with the heartfelt avowals and passions of others. I try out my warmth toward you. I listen for your response, but also listen to my own response to my initial improvisation of warmth. I'm ready to reset my attunement, as needed. Am I suddenly embarrassed by my full-volume venture toward intimacy? Or am I too halting? Sensibility is improvisational. Sometimes I'm estranged from myself. I wonder whether what I have just said to you is truly me speaking. An outflow of sensibility extends my intimacy, and I have second-order monitorings of these extensions. I'm sensible of what my warmth, mercy, or pride occasions as it extends to others. I can evaluate both its reception and its feel to me—does it "feel right"? To embody and live through religious sensibility is a continually unfolding drama of nuanced attunements and resettings.

My warmth for you is improvisational. A great conductor shapes her interpretations even as her players begin initial responses to her cues. She can't follow a rigid map for what tone, color, or tempo will come next. She responds to the resonance of the concert hall, to the alertness of her players, to her memory of past performances and of the last phrase played.

Dead religious routine is dead in the way dull concert performances are. When performance comes alive, the difference can rest on a conductor's improvisatory adjustments. Subjectivities are not isolate but inter-animating.[5] When warmth is reciprocated interpersonally, each strengthens its other. A mother's subjectivity develops overtime in tandem with her child's. The child develops a personal mode of being in relation to its mother's. Religious sensibility, too, flourishes as a nexus of outflowing and incoming intermeshing subjectivities.[6] My subjectivity is present in attunement with nature—when it speaks through thunder, trembling branches, or surf. It is attuned to literary and cultural figures, to particular lines of verse, or to architectural features of my city.

My sense of Christianity is responsive to the sensibilities of Alyosha Karamazov, or Tolstoy's Ivan Ilytch, or to sensibilities expressed in a great cathedral, not to mention Dickinson's poetry, Bach Chorales, or particular Psalms. We are not a conjugation or concatenation of objects but subjects in waxing and waning communion. Kierkegaard avers that "faith is the highest passion."[7] Passions are not just storms trapped inside mind or soul, ready to boil over. If they're sometimes that, they're also inward pointing outward, quiet or tumultuous streams joining me to things and people. They heighten and focus my concern.

If I love you, or love my God, this marks a flow of passion or heartfeltness toward targets that repay my attention. Kierkegaardian subjectivity or inwardness doesn't seal us off from the world but connects us to others and the world through the *heart*—not through cognition-only. My religious sensibility shows up as my heart flows toward children or scriptural passages about children; toward dawn or meadow, or scriptural passages about dawn or meadow; toward a sheen of things carrying a sense of the holy, the sacred, or the divine.

Graveyard sensibilities

In the middle of *Concluding Unscientific Postscript*, we find a theatrical set piece—a dramatic, or even melodramatic, graveyard scene. It presents a broadly religious-poetic sensibility.[8] Climacus, a Kierkegaardian pseudonym, reports a scene overheard, seen in a fugitive glance through leaves, as he sits on a bench at twilight. His is seated in "the garden of the dead," a cemetery most likely Copenhagen's Assistens Kirkegård.[9] The scene is not out in the wooded parklands. Nevertheless, it's sufficiently alive with nature's leafy shadows to allow Climacus to exalt in minor ecstasy over the coming of night. It's as if night carried an invitation for a "nocturnal tryst," a beautiful prelude to the more tearful tableau ahead.

Through the trees we see and hear a grandfather mourning at the grave of his son. His grandson is present. Here is the heft and pathos of life. He speaks tearfully of the senselessness of that death, and of the life that preceded it. The old man addresses the now fatherless ten-year-old. The poetry of the setting amplifies the grandfather's grief and his anguished admonition to a barely understanding grandson. The old man speaks, and the night speaks too—of yearning and heartache. The night promises

> a tryst ... with the infinite, persuaded by the night's breeze as in a monotone it repeats itself, breathing through forest and meadow, and sighing as though in search of something, urged by the distant echo in oneself of the stillness as if intimating something, urged by the sublime calm of the heavens, as if this something had been found, persuaded by the palpable silence of the dew as if this were the explanation and infinitude's refreshment, like the fecundity of a quiet night, only half understood like the night's semi-diaphanous mist.[10]

We have a somber sensibility, religiously tinted, that embraces family, the night, and the witnesses. Reading the passage energizes our own sensibilities, attuned by poetic depiction. The night carries a religious sheen. Thinking "truth is subjectivity" calls to mind truths in a testimony of love, in a heart's openness to an address from others, or from a leaf-dappled night.

This is an *intimately* sublime sensibility.[11] For Kant, the sublime would be mountains towering and violent storms where death and life hang in the balance. Our cemetery is a down-scaled sublime. Death haunts, but only in the gentle half-understood sighing of a breeze, in the "semi-diaphanous mist" of the night, in the "palpable silence of the dew." This domesticated sublime leaves us in restless repose, in a poetic-spiritual-religious sensibility, as if conveyed in a Psalm that can place us by still water.

But the night scene is also agitated. A nocturnal tryst foretells both anxiety *and* refreshment, not unlike Kant's mix of fear and pleasure as he gazes from an alpine peak. We yearn for the infinite repose of a beckoning night. Thus, a Christian might yearn for the infinite repose of a savior seen through a glass darkly. Climacus yearns for the comforting "silence of the dew." Nature "signals a kind of transcendence" that evokes "the anxiety of self-relation."[12] What is it to have one's sense of self or soul emerge in resonance with the anxious dark of the night?

Things and persons speak. A man is broken in grief. We sense a frightened grandson, a fresh grave, an anxious night, a screen of leafy boughs behind which Climacus hides and listens. This tryst with the infinite is what Kierkegaard elsewhere calls an "objective uncertainty" held in "the most passionate inwardness."[13]

> the night's breeze ... repeats itself, breathing through forest and meadow, and sighing as though in search of something, urged by the distant echo in oneself of the stillness as if intimating something.[14]

The sighing of night reflects a sighing soul, and a sighing soul reflects night—each yearning for rest signaled by silent dew. It's not as though anxiety mechanically causes the skies to spin. It's poetic fit: lightening portends a shock to the heart, and a shock to the heart portends lightening.

Death disrupts the living and puts all under judgment. Climacus has his composure stolen in the way love, beauty, or truth might steal up and overcome dull nonchalance. The sensibility in play is like a vessel stirred by the lessons of love, suffering, and communion, quite oblivious to doctrine or social conformity.

The old man fears for the soul of his son, caught up in the illusion that philosophical or historical speculation or debate about faith could substitute for being of faith. Now, through tears, he pleads with his grandson, as if to say "Beware! Beware erudite scholarly engagement." Beware losing your piety and soul to the study of history, creeds, or institutions. Scholarship about faith dances with objectivities, neglecting faith's intimate communions. An atheist, humorist, or scholar can be deaf to anguished souls in a graveyard and portents of mists.

Words stir the soul

"Self" is a center of autonomous action and decision, a person's executive functions. "Soul" is a site of receptivity, of listening to presence. Humans are both self and soul, centers of action, and centers of receptivity. The enlightenment, which has left an indelible mark, championed the self's individual liberties to the neglect of the soul's receptivities. The emergence of industrial society further advanced the reign of the self. Nature became disenchanted, mainly a resource for industry. With the disenchantment and alienation of factory work, both self and soul, dual sources of inestimable worth, took a beating. Luckily, the arts keep self and soul alive.

Religious discourse, including Kierkegaard's, delivers a *what* (*what* is said) and a *how* (*how* it is said). I can be stirred by what words *say*, merely as words—apart from the mode of delivery, the "how" of their delivery. And I can be stirred by a presence animating a person's saying, doing, thinking, or feeling. Words of love or faith can be eloquent as words in their dictionary meanings alone. I can catch this eloquence reading them silently. To present them vocally gives an added dimension to stirring words.

Delivered with passion, words are modulated by my tone of voice, by the rhythm and timbre of my delivery, and by accompanying bodily rigidity, slackness, or animation: I convey brashness, fear, or hesitation. A professional actor on stage will deliver words with a presence I can only envy. A courtroom stenographer records bare words, whatever the bearing and presence of the speaker. Being attuned to presence in delivery is like hearing or missing subtleties in musical phrasing.

Words from a text can stir us along the dimensions of both the *what* and the *how*. If I focus, deadpan, on the words alone, I maximize the *what*. If I tune to their presence, I am a soul—receptive to presence. I let words sweep me up or crush me. Scriptural words, or Kierkegaard's, have spoken weight, impact, pitch, and rhythm. They can have overtones, bite, softness, or volume. They can express a lilt and spice of life.

Not all religious or philosophical writers want to make their words come alive. A historian of religion can safely leave the "passionate how" out of the picture. We can peel away what Wittgenstein calls the "spirit" of writing.[15] But any who write from a religious sensibility will want to convey the tang of life, the grief and intimacy of the old man in a graveyard.

Unfortunately, Kierkegaard's *Postscript* can be received as flat opinion, raising flat questions and launching spiritless debate. Better, these passages can arrive lively and animated, full of passion, humming like a chorister treading home from church, or crackling like punch lines from a comic. Words in motion deliver the crash and purr of a worldly presence, in its mysterious coming-to-be. Passionate attunement to living words infuses religions sensibility.

As we've heard in Chapter 2, Heidegger, much indebted to Kierkegaard, writes that "Philosophy necessarily stands in the radiance of what is beautiful and in the throes of what is holy."[16] The beautiful and the holy address our poetic-religious-philosophical sensibilities. We've heard an historian writing about the philosopher F. H. Bradley:

> [He] is trying to write the drama of life as it is, with all the stage directions, to express, not only what the actors do, say, think, and feel, but also what

they are expressing. If one could succeed, the result would be life itself, completely known. We would see why, we would understand ... we would feel the very tang of life itself.[17]

Too easily, we can think of Kierkegaard—and religion—as opinionated and didactic, exploiting scripture to convey a message. There are beliefs or propositions: "God is love," "Truth is Subjectivity." And there are questions: "What is the afterlife?" "What is sin?" Kierkegaard might ask: "What is truth?" or "Is there a teleological suspension of the ethical?" Yet one can inhabit a deep religious sensibility and remain profoundly unknowing about ever-so-many propositions and messages in a religion. Kierkegaard's writings stir the soul in ways that are radiantly present and strangely elusive. His poetic philosophy gives us "the tang of life" at the cusp of coming-to-be. He offers the radiant presence of an ever-unfolding world both holy and beautiful.[18] Much of his writing is theater. Scripture contains rules and facts, but also dramas of creation, theaters of good and evil, tales of reverence and irreverence, of crimes and punishments. Drama embraces poetry, myth, and parable.

Kierkegaard's ideas are on stage, where he tries "to express, not only what [his] actors do, say, think, and feel, but also what they are expressing [in that doing, saying, thinking, and feeling]." To bathe in a religious sensibility is to let the presence of words shine. Presence conveys amazement and recoil. Like a whisper or cry, his words suspend an exclusively cognitive tracking of sentences—a good thing, for then there's an opening for revelation. Grounding power bespeaks sensibility, wherein we open to the radiant goodness of goods. As the rose radiates its beauty without a *Why*, or my love radiates an allure without *Why*, so am I grounded in a religious sensibility without *Why*. There is no meaningful life without radiance.

8
Who is Kierkegaard?

He lived in Copenhagen from 1813 to 1855, in the backwaters of European culture. The centers were Paris, Berlin, and London, but he soon put Copenhagen on the map. Along with Hegel, Marx, and Nietzsche, Kierkegaard is indispensable for understanding nineteenth-century theology and philosophy. His texts became a priceless inheritance for Heidegger, Ibsen, Kafka, Sartre, Buber, Ortega, Rilke, and Tillich.

Partially in response to Kierkegaard, "Existentialism" emerged between the wars in Germany and France in the work of Jaspers and Heidegger. Those who sensed a crisis of spirit, not least in religion, were attracted. Kierkegaard's psychosocial analyses of "the crowd," of dread and anxiety, of love and hope and self-deception provided a diagnosis of those years of tumult and despair as the rise of Nazism hung ominously over everything. Kierkegaard's subtle mix of skepticism, hope, and social critique was poignantly alluring. His cutting irony, psychological acuity, and astounding intelligence make him irresistible, then and today.

Disquieting, elusive

From his earliest journal, Kierkegaard pleads for knowledge that will "come alive in me," for knowledge that has subjective weight.[1] He refuses a university career in part because he wants more than objective knowledge. He needs knowledge that will quicken an intimate self-recognition keyed to folds of his existence that he alone can access—alone, in communion with books, memories, imagined and actual readers, friends, a brother, a father, a girl he couldn't marry.[2]

Kierkegaard has regard for his readers—for their subjective, personal being. He prods me to drop *exclusive* attention to the world-historical and to starkly impersonal objectivity. This is disquieting. To confront my subjectivity is disquieting. Paradoxically, tracking my subjectivity can make me elusive to myself—I slip out of sight. And it can make Kierkegaard elusive.

To take up with my being-as-a-subject is not solipsism. My subjectivity develops through relations. Kierkegaard's subjectivity develops in relation to his mentors—to Socrates, but also to Cervantes and Hamlet, as well as to his family and neighbors. My own mentors might include Socrates, Kierkegaard, and Hamlet, as well as those marvelous Kierkegaardian inventions, the pseudonyms. Among many others, consider the immortal Johannes de silentio, who pens *Fear and Trembling*, or that humorous anti-professor, Johannes Climacus, who pens the *Concluding Unscientific Postscript*.

He aims to disquiet rather than to argue for doctrine. He works from Christian, Socratic, Romantic, and Ironic standpoints, and can be called a Poet or Philosopher, a Preacher or Pundit—any of these at a moment's notice, or all rolled into one. Appearing in so many guises he eludes our grasp. And we may sense that we may be just as elusive to ourselves.

In 1843, Kierkegaard published *Either/Or, Fear and Trembling*, and *Repetition*—each of monumental impact. But what exactly is their point? At first glance, the reader of *Either/Or* confronts a radical choice between two ways of life. The first path, evoked in "Either," is the life of an aesthete, artist, or bohemian, contemptuous of social institutions and the claims of ethics and religion. Shall I choose *this*? Perhaps the "Or" of *Either/Or* is preferable. The second volume gives us letters from an upright member of society, a Judge, who shows the emptiness of a vague aesthetic, nonethical life of melancholy and despair. The Judge summons "A," the anonymous author of volume one, to make a life choice, to choose to become himself. This means choosing social roots and obligations.

Kierkegaard's first great work leaves much up in the air. For one thing, the aesthete is attractive—perhaps more attractive than the Judge. He writes "The Diary of the Seducer" (often published separately), and "The Musical Erotic" on Mozart's *Don Giovanni*—not to mention a number of other short essays and sets of aphorisms. If the aesthete can produce these gems, why does he need to "get a life," to "choose himself"? Why isn't he just fine as he is? Despite the Judge's moralistic judgment, perhaps "A" has *already* "chosen himself"—chosen to be precisely the aesthete that his self-righteous accuser disapproves of. He might enjoy a creative freedom the Judge will never know. And we won't know, because in *Either/Or* the aesthete is not allowed a rebuttal. There is another possibility. The aesthete might be an upright individual and just write up an alternative life for amusement. To imagine a seducer is not to be one; a decent person can sketch unethical lives. Does Kierkegaard favor the Judge, who defends ethical-religious life? Perhaps he believes the notion of "objective superiority" has no grip here, and he wants to leave the subjective choice between two ways of life up to me.[3] Yet if reason can't show one way of life superior to the other, life choice is arbitrary. We endorse nihilism or value-relativism: an "aesthetic" outcome wins out.

Kierkegaard delights in these existential ambiguities. To make matters worse, *Either/Or* ends with the sketch of a third life option. A parson appears. His sermon follows the exhortations of the Judge. Life options now include the religious as well as the aesthetic and the ethical. We have an "either-or-or." This is the germ of a three-stage theory of human existence. Two years later Kierkegaard will write *Stages on Life's Way*, also under a pseudonym. Does he take the religious way of life to be best, is he pulled in three directions at once, or is he leaving it all up to me—to us?

A philosopher or theologian normally will make clear what position is being advanced. Otherwise, how can we make an assessment? Yet Kierkegaard ducks any clear resolution to the standoff among life options. They are just laid before us. And pseudonyms mask *his* considered judgment. We have "Victor Emeritus" responsible for *Either/Or*, and Johannes de silentio responsible for *Fear and Trembling*, and Johannes Climacus responsible for *Philosophical Crumbs*. But where is Kierkegaard himself hiding?[4]

There are unstated reasons to be elusive. If he wrote as a professor, pastor, or celebrity he'd add false authority to his books. Literature or philosophy should be evaluated apart from its author's notoriety or position. We admire Homer, or *Genesis*, or the *Vedas*, knowing nothing about the persons who wrote them. Pseudonyms insure Kierkegaard's *biographical* absence. As important, the device enacts the truth, or partial truth, that persons are multiple, a kind of theater. "The" self is a cast of many characters or roles—like the array of pseudonyms. This is a circus or carnival identity. Pseudonyms are both teasing entertainment and serious theater of selfhood. We ask why he chooses just this name, or plays hide and seek just this way, and why his religious, sermon-like discourses (published regularly alongside his pseudonymous works) carry the name "Kierkegaard." He's a pestering, provocative, elusive, seductive Socrates.

Spiritual crisis

A second great work of 1843 is *Fear and Trembling*. Johannes de silentio improvises on the biblical account of Abraham taking Isaac to Mt. Moriah to be sacrificed. Nothing in Kierkegaard is more grippingly elusive than his rendering of this tale.

Most readers assume there will be a defense of Abraham. But Johannes just wants to understand him—and he says over and over that he can't. How can you defend what you can't understand? Johannes asks (without answering) if there is a "teleological suspension of the ethical" in play. If Abraham rightfully sets out to kill Isaac, then ethics must be idle—suspended. At the last minute an angel tells Abraham to put down his knife. Yet he seems prepared to commit what any sane person would call murder—unless God sets ethics aside.

Surely Kierkegaard knows the danger of postulating a God who expects us to act unethically. *Fear and Trembling* apparently lets God and ethics collide. Kant said Abraham is mistaken. He should have doubted it was God who was speaking. But that rewrites the Bible. Ethics would reign as an absolute even God couldn't contravene. Is Kant correct? Does Kierkegaard advocate an irrational and immoral submission to God's will? Many philosophers scorn *Fear and Trembling*. But Kierkegaard (or Johannes) presents moral-religious ambiguity, undecidability, in the *Genesis* story. He does not support irrationality or immorality. We're left with massive, frightening ambiguity. Will God or Ethics reign?

Ambiguous biblical tales can be valuable the way ambiguous dreams can be. The portraits of four Abrahams (and, indeed, of four mothers) at the beginning of *Fear and Trembling* are placed in a dreamy, fairy tale ambiance. The section begins, "Once there was a man who remembered the beautiful tale he heard as a child ... "[5] The tale, of course, is a nightmare, not "a beautiful tale." But even nightmares don't advocate the horrors they depict. Abraham leads us to profound reflections, even as he baffles. Socrates also leads us to irresolution and ignorance, nevertheless, enthralled. The Abraham tale is not alone among Biblical passages depicting a morally ambiguous God. God lets Satan afflict Job; He has a sudden impulse to kill Moses[6]; He lets his son be crucified. These tales defy and beg for interpretation. They leave us ignorant. They don't commend the glorious horrors they depict.

Let's suppose that in yielding to the Whirlwind Job comes to acknowledge a Creation profoundly unconcerned with his well-being. (We've considered this in our discussion of Henry Bugbee's meditations). Still, we'd wonder how the Creator in Job lines up with a God of Justice. Similarly, we wonder how the God whose angel stays Abraham's hand lines up with the God asking Abraham to raise his knife? Is Johannes de silentio right, that Abraham has double consciousness, convinced both that Isaac will be lost and not be lost, given up and received back? Dreams and children's stories—remember, "once there was a man ... "—tolerate such contractions. We tarry with them, fascinated and disturbed.

Kierkegaard never pronounces, "One must always obey God, even when a command is unethical," and he never pronounces, "When a command is unethical, one must disobey." He displays quandaries. A line of questioning is opened and *left* open. We inherit a searing Socratic ignorance.

There are other issues raised—and left hanging. Early on Johannes de silentio gives us four pictures of what might have been going through Abraham's mind. None pass the test of faith. In one, Abraham's hand trembles in despair. Three of the Abrahams obey yet fail the test. That's not the only cause of wonder. In a stroke of innovative genius, Johannes appends under each of the four portraits counter-portraits of a mother weaning her child.

We took faith to be a bridge that gets Abraham through catastrophic crisis. Now we find faith to be a bridge that gets a Mother-Abraham through the mundane trial of weaning. Mothers bring faith into the ordinary. It appears Johannes sees that it takes faith to countenance sacrificing a son and takes as much faith to countenance weaning a son. This transposition from sacrifice to weaning opens the possibility that Abraham's trial is less about extinguishing Isaac's life than about the necessary separation of father and son. For spiritual maturity, the father must be weaned from his son, and the son weaned from his father. Perhaps also Abraham must be weaned from the presumption that God is—*simply*—a benevolent provider and protector. He has concerns beyond the child's ken.

Weaning is mundane, and mundane faith is pervasive in *Fear and Trembling*. Johannes finds a knight of faith disguised, not as a weaning mother, but as an ordinary shopkeeper. He finds a knight of resignation (not yet a knight of faith) disguised as a young man suffering unrequited love. As de silentio puts it, these improvisations show "the sublime in the pedestrian." We apparently move light years from the horror on Moriah, or interpret that horror through pedestrian figures of faith, including mothers weaning. The Moriah story is no more irrational nor immoral than the weaning stories, or the story of the whistling shopkeeper strolling home for an expected dish of lamb.

Almost as an aside, Johannes slips in a serviceable definition of faith. Faith is managing crisis by "giving up and getting back."[7] Surrender precedes gift. A mother gives up, surrenders, her infant and gets it back. Abraham gives up Isaac and gets him back. "Giving up" is resigning one's self-absorbed claims to control all aspects of life, or to control others whose lives are woven into ours. The second movement is finally to enjoy the gift of a world or a loved one returned. We get back what we had surrendered—now, without possessiveness. Abraham and mothers give up their most prized "possession"—then get it back, freed of possessiveness. Johannes de Silentio's knight of resignation gives up his beloved but doesn't qualify for her return: he accepts her loss, period. He can dance the "giving up" but not the "getting back," which requires hope and trust against all reasonable expectation.

Recollection, revelation

Kierkegaard's third great work from 1843, *Repetition*, begins with a disquisition by "Constantine Constantius" on a quasi-metaphysical concept he calls "repetition." It means getting back from an open future what one has lost. When a musical section is followed by a repeat sign, the first run-through doesn't leave us at a loss. In "taking the repeat," or "going back to the top," we get back what, at first ending, seemed like a loss, a finish. Yet we get it all back.

The second half of the book contains letters between Constantine and a young man who is waiting—despairingly—for love to arrive (or return or "repeat"). He wants Job's apocalyptic moment when the heavens part, the

Voice from the Whirlwind descends, and he's bestowed meaning after all was lost. Nothing less will sooth his hapless existence. Wildly sentimental, he likens his suffering to Job's. The comparison is comical, like raising a parallel between Abraham's crisis and the worry of the shopkeeper over whether his wife will offer him roast lamb—just as Abraham, on Moriah, received a lamb that released him from pain. *Repetition* hearkens the gift of a world restored, of finding one's feet once again, after having lost them.

Threading through *Fear and Trembling* and *Repetition* is a pervasive aura of Socratic seeking, ignorance, and wonder; of yearnings for satisfying life; of transpositions of biblical catastrophe into the everyday. Faith is never "irrational blind obedience" or creedal belief in deity. Faith is a capacity to receive a crisis-weathering gift, to lose a life that we may find it—a knack for finding joy even amidst catastrophe in hope for "repetition," for "receiving back."

A mammoth and elusive tome

Philosophical Crumbs (1844) and *Concluding Unscientific Postscript* (1846) are not claimed by Kierkegaard. The hide-and-seek of pseudonymous authorship continues. *Postscript* is signed off as the work of Johannes Climacus. Kierkegaard avoids academic works of philosophy or theology, avoids plain and simple poetry, drama, or the novel, and avoids direct responsibility for his words. He's also a master of crossbreeding. What looks like a very serious academic tome—the 600-page *Postscript*—is in many ways a satire of philosophical-theological tomes. What looks like a work in psychology, *The Concept of Anxiety*, is an investigation of sin. What looks like a literary miscellany, the varied papers in *Either/Or*, hints at a ladder from aesthetic to ethical to religious spheres of existence.

Literature and theory, philosophy, theology, and psychology arrive in a stew. He shifts us from sorting things by socially objective categories—finding this to be psychology; this, philosophy; this, irony, and so forth—to seeking words with subjective resonance for *me*. He wants *me* to wrestle subjectively with this writing, whatever the genre, and to wrestle with the *absence* of genre. Religious thinking is mixed with literary innovation: he launches a book called *Prefaces* that contains nothing but prefaces. His literary efforts are seasoned with philosophical acumen, and his philosophy rings with the religious. He's a defender of the faith and a critic of its institutions. He defies categorization.

Kierkegaard's 1844 treatise, *Philosophical Crumbs or a Crumb of Philosophy*, mocks weighty tomes and is self-mocking: he offers only crumbs swept from the high table for consumption by the lowly. A Socratic view of truth as recollection faces the Christian view of truth as revelation. For Socrates, truth is within us, waiting to be dredged from memory. For Christianity, truth is a revelatory impact that makes us new persons without pasts to dredge.

Subjective truth

Like *Philosophical Crumbs*, the 1846 *Postscript* mocks academic tomes. Consider the full title: *Concluding Unscientific Postscript to the Philosophical Crumbs: a Mimic Pathetic Dialectical Compilation: an Existential Contribution*. We've considered the title at length in Chapter 3, "The tang of life." This is a "postscript" (or afterthought) that runs six times the length of the text it's appended to. The age aspires to be triumphantly scientific yet here's something avowedly unscientific. The postscript dares to be "concluding," ringing down the curtain on otherwise interminable discussions. A *mimic* compilation forecasts farce, satire, or humor. A *pathetic* compilation foretells tragedy and pathos. A *dialectical* compilation is something after the style of Hegel. A *compilation* is a loose-knit assembly of thoughts, not a system or dissertation. Finally, an *existential contribution* is a gift meant to help me brace and clarify myself.

For many, Kierkegaard's fate is linked to the *Postscript* idea that "truth is subjectivity." A person's existence or subjectivity resonates in the silent resonance of faith, in the agency (and passivity) one has in relations to oneself, others, an environing world and God—and anything of great value. The truth of subjectivity is the truth that we are subjectivities exposed and responsive to other subjectivities whose co-ordinate existence is the weave of our worlds.

Kierkegaard's "subjectivity" is not a partiality in statements or reports, thus a defect. Everyday Kierkegaardian subjectivity affords flowing, unbiased contact with the world. There's no bias in loving your child—it's not unfair or prejudiced. It's just straightforward (we hope) and your legitimate link to another. Persons, subjects (non-objects) contest truths in pursuit of what's real. I can be subjectively engaged in pursuing objective truth; I hope I am. It's *my* passionate pursuit. I want to know the objective truth about Kierkegaard's claims for subjectivity. Attaining objectivity does not erase the subjectivity that initiated the pursuit and that celebrates its success. You can subjectively admire an objective map of the terrain.

"Subjectivity" is not an isolated Cartesian atom of consciousness—sundered from others, isolated from the world. In my subjectivity, I am in *this* town, at *this* address, happy or unhappy in *this* family and *this* job, disgusted or delighted by *this* evening's news. I am a "me" open to the world and to others; I am being-here, *Dasein*. The truth of subjectivity is the inescapability of personal immersion in life and is a practical appeal. We need to pierce through the illusion of merely objective existence, a no man's land instilling despair. Some truths *matter* to me, and their mattering is their subjectivity.[8]

Irony

Kierkegaard's university dissertation is *The Concept of Irony with Constant Reference to Socrates (1841)*. He confessed late in life that he was always Socratic.

I suspect he was nearly always ironic—except with regard to his attachment to Socrates. Irony is the capacity to simultaneously see the underside and topside of our aspirations and evaluations. We grasp both our recurrent failures and our bracing victories. This "doubleness" of irony might be the fundamental structure of evaluative consciousness for modern subjects.

Irony can be episodic rather than global. Kierkegaard, like Socrates, is a master of the ironic wisecrack or quip. He can take a jaded view of what his audience takes as a happy or normal perception. He notes priests preaching Gospel poverty while dressed like kings. He can reverse what his audience sees as jaded—in a quip, he considers becoming a master thief. Reversing evaluations through ironic wisecracks is a staple of comedy and banter: we ironically flip commonplace views of gender, age, ethnicity, size, family, eating, kissing, or priests. Irony can be serious even as it triggers laughter.

But irony can also be a sustained reflective stance. Kierkegaard can take a backward step affording a sweeping view of a large sector of life and put it under ironic scrutiny. He'll see its upsides and downsides simultaneously. Love life, sports life, political life, religious life, or humanity in general, can be viewed globally through the lens of a cultivated irony. Double vision replaces hard-edge one-dimensional judgment. To think "preachers are corrupt" can be wooden and un-ironic. To tell a tale of parsonage tomfoolery that concedes parsons some dignity can be a forgiving, bracing irony—a gift of double vision.

An ironic Kierkegaard could depict parsonage tomfoolery yoked to a salutary view of a priestly contribution—say, at funerals. Irony cultivates binocular evaluation. Think of it: Socrates believes in the examined life yet won't examine Diotima's view of love.

A backward step toward a broad ironic perspective puts one at a distance from action. If it becomes chronic, and negative—demonic—it stalls action, drifting toward boredom or melancholic passivity. This is the framework for Kierkegaard's criticism of the life of the aesthete: it's limitlessly negative and one-dimensional. But a twofold ironic perspective can be bracing and vibrant rather than negative and demonic. Under a bracing ironic gaze, life can veer toward joy and delight—or perhaps, serenity. Socrates can live the upside of his life in the city despite acute awareness of the city's miserable downsides.

Demonic irony freezes action. It sours morale, indulging a regressive cycle that buries a capacity to see *upsides*—along with downsides. To relentlessly subvert one's better perceptions, criticizing this project and that, is the death of irony and of living. Irony becomes cynicism or despair. A full life can harbor a bracing irony where downsides are only dominant episodically. And ironic living (as opposed to ironic remarks) occasionally shelves the double perspective—say as Socrates gives way wholeheartedly to Diotima. There are no rules for when the backward step will be of service, and when it should be overridden.

At our best, we improvise in the arenas of meaning and action, having a knack for when and how to allow reflection's backward step. When bad things happen, we improvise escapes from *prolonged* downslides. Irony lies at the heart of Socratic religion, and it's also, I'd hazard, at the heart of Christian religion. To see life under the withering judgment of sin is the wound of Christian existence. That wound is ironically married to its opposite, restorative love and forgiveness.

Paradox and indirection

Both formal philosophy and apologetic theology should be silenced before Abraham on Moriah, or Christ either suffering on the cross or rising from the dead. The Incarnation is a disaster for thought. It's an absolute paradox. It asks us to affirm the God-Man, which sounds like affirming a tree-rock or an all-powerful powerlessness. For Kierkegaard, "the absolute paradox" or "the absurd" counteracts the presumptions that the world is an intelligible whole or is developing through Hegelian dialectic toward rational unity. More concretely, there's clearly something "absurd" or discordant about Abraham's situation on Moriah or Christ's on Calvary.

Indirect communication is called for when listener and speaker face something rationally discordant or elusive. Here, subjective feeling, mood, and interest are essential vectors of communication. Direct communication is suited for the transfer of objective content, theory or information, or for making simple requests or promises. Another, equally important channel is "indirect communication." This refers to the transfer of the subjective underlay to objective communication. I can say "I'm going to church" in a tone of distain, anger, indifference, devotion, or giddiness. The tone is a subjective modality underlying the objective information transferred. Communicated tone can arrive loud and clear but Kierkegaard will call that tone "indirect" to distinguish it from communication of simple content. One's belief in Christ is conveyed in indirect communication. To attest to belief is not reporting a dull fact about me. The attestation conveys my spirit and soul. Indirect communication can be on target or off-center. I can't just say "I believe in Jesus Christ" in a monotone, leaving my heart dead. In this case, an appropriate indirect communication includes a heartfelt tone free of anger, spite, or mockery. *How* the utterance of belief is conveyed is as important as *what* is believed. The "how" is indirectly communicated.

Relationality

Sickness unto Death (1849) portrays the self as a pattern of interweaving relationships. It is not a Cartesian mental substance, nor a substance of any sort. It is not a Zen-like nothingness, not a Nietzschean useful fiction, nor a dubious cultural construction in need of deconstruction. It's a constellation of internal relationships, an ensemble. Each member of the ensemble acts, listens, and responds like the members of a chamber music group. Kierkegaard puts the matter austerely: "The self is a relation that relates to itself, and in that relation, relates to another."[9]

Melodic lines weave in and out of a constellation made of nothing but other weaving lines. Any member of a string quartet relates to herself, relates to her fellow players and also to the constellation of sound they produce. Each relates to others and to "another"—we might say the composer's conception of the piece, or the "form" of the piece. If we are theologians, we might say that the ensemble relates to itself and then as a whole to God.[10] We needn't ask whether "the self" is body or soul, corporeal or mental, any more than we ask whether waterfalls are water or rock face.

We find in this formula for selfhood six paired self-factors: freedom-necessity, time-eternity, and infinite-finite. Each member of this ever-emerging self-ensemble can be interpreted as a need, project, or good in tensed opposition to a contrary. A need for immersion in time, for the temporal bustle of the city, is opposed to a need to escape bustle, to enter a timeless solitude. Each member has a correlative good. My need for detachment or freedom is a need for the good of detachment or freedom. Among the bequeathed goods I might await and cultivate are justice, creativity, athletic prowess or camaraderie; bravery, honor, service, family, or contemplation. These possibilities appear as strands of an identity not yet my own.

The self-relation can await or enjoy a relation to another. A pathos-ridden youth, in *Repetition*, awaits a gift of self. He is ready to relate to a soul mate or the self he might be. In acknowledging the warmth of a child's smile, I relate to another. I *am* that relation to a child. The other is a gift I cannot choose or command, just as the musical line from the viola is beyond my choice or command—even as I, a chamber player, will become myself only as I relate to this other.

Authenticity

Self-relations are always open to revisions and assessments internal to their unfolding. Kant saw the essence of our humanity in our capacity to step back and add an "I think" to any mental state. Kierkegaard sees the essence of our humanity as a capacity to step back and ask, "Am I really this?" Thus, I evaluate a need, desire, project, or correlative good.

Arrays of commitments or desires are open to evaluation and revision as a self-ensemble improvises its way into a future it can call its own. An authentic self is fairly constantly under negotiation and revision. The process is as familiar as weighing alternatives. One's family needs more time; one's career can be cut back; one has been lax in attention to relatives. Humans are an issue for themselves. Authenticity comes into play as persons care for or take a stand on what they are about and what they will be. My friend is vulnerable to the conflicting demands of being a sister, a pilot, a cancer survivor. She evaluates whether she has been, and will be, true to herself in her complexity. This is not easy. She may downplay her self-as-survivor or her self-as-sister yet hide this downplaying from herself. Perhaps she blushes with shame, suspicious that she has betrayed the sister she would be.

There is no room here for a "super-self," an executive self that conducts the negotiations and evaluations. My finite needs qualify and indirectly assess my infinite hope; my momentary anger qualifies my lasting compassion. There is no digging deeper than the ensemble of relations that reaches out expressively to others.

Abyss or grounding power

Kierkegaard appeals frankly to God as the power that rescues the self from an abyss of flailing relations. This divine grounding power is also the source of all goods to which the self might healthily relate. But Anti-Climacus—our pseudonym in *Sickness*—also adopts a less religiously committed stance. After all, an "establishing power" to whom one relates might be one's history or a concatenation of one's virtues. Or one might be grounded in a mysterious sense of dependence. George Pattison writes, "for those in the stream of

Schleiermacher's thought [as Kierkegaard was] the choice is not: do I have to be a fundamentalist believer or a secularist, but: how can I best articulate this mysterious moment in which I realize my life is given to me, as if from another."[11] That moment when I feel that my life is "given to me, as if from another" is both a moment of groundlessness, and of awe and grateful wonder.

Groundlessness is felt in the experience of futility in endlessly seeking layers under layers, grounds under grounds, reasons beneath everything. This seeking is what Kant calls a "need of reason," a need, it seems, that can never be satisfied; yet the prospect of a dizzying regress is unacceptable. We want an Ultimate Power or a Final Good to stop regressions. A regression-stopping absolute would wipe out my ignorance or perhaps my absurdity. But there is another possibility. In the instance cited by Pattison, I do not find in my ignorance a frightening abyss but instead a wondrous rest from my worries. I find patience in the sense that "my life is mysteriously given me." It is a peace *beyond* reasons or grounds. Paradoxically, I can find myself grounded, ultimately steady—while being utterly without grounds.

When I ask for grounds for a belief, I ask for groundings-in-reasons. To have a ground, or be grounded, is to have a reason. But sometimes I receive a handhold, an assurance that is not a reason but a felt-security or groundedness I can't elaborate as a reason. The shopkeeper knight of faith from *Fear and Trembling* enjoys grounding—grounding-as-assurance—with no access to *reasons*. I enjoy a child's smile and immediately feel myself grounded in its wonder. That's not arriving at a doubt-stopping *reason*. For no worldly reason, Socrates listens to Diotima, *groundlessly grounded* in her allure. Demonic irony leaves one staring into an abyss. Bracing or salvific irony leaves one assured. Diotima, like a child's smile, is a groundless ground.

A picture of faith as "grounding power"—the sense that the world is welcoming rather than a dizzying mess—is implicit in the image of the jaunty shopkeeper.[12] This knight of faith strolls home for dinner, taking delight in all that his eyes take in. He is implicitly grounded, assured quite beyond reasons.

Johannes de silentio avers that the knight is "secure to take pleasure in [the world]"—he is "living happily and joyfully." His faith is an implicit power grounding an assured and happy living, despite lack of justifying reasons.[13] He doesn't write a *lawyerly defense* of such "establishing power" or grounding assurance. This would push away the wonder of a grounding assurance utterly free of reason. He closes the door on digressions.

Socrates repeatedly turns to myths, images, and fantastical stories at key points, knowing that arguments only go so far. One does not come to awe, love, wonder, or radiant assurance through reasoning. "Grounding power" bespeaks the radiant goodness of goods-without-reason. The rose radiates beauty without a *Why*. When assurance is present, I too am grounded without a *Why*. To live in faithful assurance is not to assert that something transcendent exists. The beauty of this rose floats free of anything deeper. Its beauty sweeps all need for reasons brusquely aside.

I can mention "establishing power" along with a full confession of ignorance with regard to any explication of a power that establishes the love or beauty or holiness that supports me. We welcome wonders afloat, despite (and alongside) ignorance. In a life full of loss, lack, and desolation, there's no need to apologize for rejoicing in available wonders. This is welcoming the persistence of groundless yet grounding joy and delight.[14]

9
Kierkegaard, seduction, and circus identity

An "objective" view of Christianity—it's history, creeds, and so forth—isn't worth much in Kierkegaard's opinion. He satirizes "the assistant professor" who prattles on about Christian Theology. The assistant is good at outlining arguments and historical overviews, but he never considers his own *existential relationship* to these things. He's a talking head. In no way is he related to William Stringfellow's circus performers:

> In the circus, one person walks on a wire fifty feet above the ground, … another, hangs in the air by the heels, one upholds twelve in a human pyramid, another is shot from a cannon. The performer is freed from consignment to death.[1]

The assistant professor is not "freed from consignment to death." He's already dead.

My host wants to hear how I've been *changed* by Kierkegaard. He wants a *subjective* sense of my philosophical ventures: what's it been like, subjectively, to have been seduced by Kierkegaard over the years.

Well, subjectively speaking, I'm a circus of rude interruptions, reveries, calls from the past, and resets, half way between angst and salvation. This is a short diary of the seduced (*Moi!*). (A Kierkegaard title is "Diary of the Seducer.") Like any good seducer, he addresses my particularity, my personal angst and joy. I'm not one of a crowd or a cipher caught up in the spirit of the age. He gives attention exclusively to *me*—which is both flattering and frightening.

Identities

Just for a moment, let me be a talking head, an "assistant professor." Here are four strings of identity: File identity, Bodily identity, Socio-political-cultural identity, and Existential identity.

File identity—my name with code numbers for tax collectors, passport offices, motor vehicles departments, university payrolls, and administrators.

Bodily identity—my height is more stable than my weight. I have footprints as well as fingerprints. There's a distinctive lilt to my walk, and a distinctive timbre to my voice. I'm an envelope of flesh and a plumber's delight. I lack a linebacker's body. My vocal chords are flexible flesh.

Socio-political-cultural identity—I'm part Irish, part Mainer with dashes of Berkeley counter-culture, and an ersatz New York intellectual. I'm not a Slovakian skier or fashion model or Russian oligarch. I could be a Concord Saunterer or a protesting tax delinquent.

Existential identity—Here, I'm an unruly, shifting sense of presence-to-myself manifest in decisive acts, and in fleeting memories that get bundled narratively, and in anticipations of what I might be tomorrow. The existential "I" who marched at MLK's funeral is not the existential "I" who joined the woman's march this last January. (The "socio-political I is pretty much the same.) The "existential me" who reads Kierkegaard in Yafa is not the "me" who reads a paper in Minnesota.

I had hoped that identity would be singular and therefore simple. But it's not. My file identity, bodily identity, and socio-political-cultural identity keep me dressed properly—or at least recognizably—in public. My existential me is not dressed for public view. It's a *me-from-inside,* a presence as I cheer my granddaughter's water polo shots, or face down a bear with my son in Yosemite. My existential identity is present as I plunge into the circus of my long-term Kierkegaard affair.

Existential identity

An existential *act* is often an identity-maker. I march in a woman's rally or light a candle for a friend on the day of the dead. In those moments I just *am* (existentially) those discrete acts. On the other hand, my marching might be *proforma*, not existential at all. Often the "existential me" is not condensed in a discrete act, or a discriminate presence for others. It can be present as a scattering of reveries, a "me-yet-to-be congealed." If Sartre loves the definitive act, Kierkegaard loves, in addition, a "me" floating as memories of what I've *been* and as imaginings of what I *might* be.

My existential identity is varied like scenes from a circus. And I live what Cora Diamond calls "difficult reality." She asks us to consider a living room photo. It elicits warmth and wonder at a handsome young man pictured in his prime. In a split second this reality shifts. The photo now elicits deep grief. That young man's vibrant life was cut short by a World War.

Both radiant promise and unmitigated grief flow from the single, nicely framed picture. In my bones I feel both realities—the reality of a blossoming youth and the reality of a tragic death. My own reality becomes difficult, double. I have conflicting feelings responsive to the dual reality before me. It's an understatement to say that if we think of an image of the Crucifixion, we have difficult reality many times over. Is the scene one of hope or one of despair?

Kierkegaard gives me tools to handle my difficult reality—my multiple realities. These include irony, humor, pseudonymity, paradox, Socratic evasions, and Socratic inquisitions. But let me start with the difficulties of

Kierkegaard's depictions of Abraham—the father of faith—in his trial on Moriah: God asks him to sacrifice his son.

Multiplicities

Kierkegaard doesn't believe in pat interpretations. There's not a *single* Abraham in his book *Fear and Trembling*, but *four* reveries of four *possible* fathers of faith. Each reverie gives a way Abraham could have failed as a man of faith. And then, to deepen the puzzle, he gives us four associated reveries of Abraham as *Mother*. Is a mother weaning her infant likened to Abraham weaning Isaac— or being weaned from overdependence on God? All eight images attune me to identity complexities. The several Abrahams and mothers mimic the dispersed "me" who picked up *Fear & Trembling* fifty years ago, when I couldn't figure out what was going on. Now I know that "the answer" is that there are *no easy answers*. Any Abraham or Abraham-mother worth savoring, I now see, is a tormented enigma slouching through inconclusive identities. These eight stories are, in their way, beautiful. Rilke says beauty is the beginning of terror.[3]

Abraham is a multiplicity. I am a multiplicity: the father confronting a bear, the soloist playing slightly out of tune, the scholar making sense of "an existential contribution." These self-images provide multiple "me-s" that are problematically linked to others. The "me" who looks at photos from my past is slightly altered with each new photo observed. I'm a difficult reality.

Who am I?

A flaneur, promenading with him through paragraphs or streets or memories. I mull reveries of father-and-son tromping Tuolumne Meadows, aware of bears. I cheer my granddaughter rifling shots in her water polo meets. SK encourages my reveries as a lover of souls, far away and close by, of toddlers and friends, here and there. My existential circus gets unmasked as phases of a difficult reality—not unlike the inharmonious voices of my friend Kierkegaard's multiple pseudonyms. The "I" that I am arises in glancing bits and pieces.[4]

There are exquisitely existential celebratory moments: "Here I stand, I can do no other." "Here we stand, we outfoxed the bear." Resolution at that point upstages gossamer possibilities. Think of the multiple "me-s" that awaited as possibilities! Which would be realized at a bear encounter? A fleeing me, fighting me, nonchalant me, paralyzed me? I ponder "me-s" amidst love, shame, anger, and a thousand other moods and presences. The Dane leaves me hanging: to hide or not to hide—or to resolve decisively.

Over the decades I've succumbed to Kierkegaard's wiles—dialectically and lyrically, comically and pathetically, through zillions of scenarios. I'm bewitched by an endless raconteur, a Socratic inquisitor, a theatrical prompter.

Mondays: I realize that I'll never outlive my existential challenges, nor escape being forever an enigma to myself.

Tuesdays: I learn my despair needn't be terminal: I can morph toward an existential hide-and-seek, an indispensable coping mechanism. I can mimic his mimic-ironic-pathetic excursions. Late night terrors can morph toward adventures.

Wednesdays: he whispers that even classroom stints can be laced with humor, paradox, and theatrical pseudonymity.

Thursdays: I'm reminded that humor, paradox, theatricality, and pseudonymity aren't just evasions but part and parcel of living multiple lives within lives: solitary life morphs toward romantic life, family life humors temple life, musical life invades body-maintenance life. A sense of me emerges from a circus of transience and multiplicity—from clowns, dialectical high-wire acts, pathos, paradox, and irony, from inwardness and pseudonymity.

Fridays: Books. I notice details: he lingers with graveyard night mists, with throwaway *Crumbs*; with *Either/Ors* and *Fears and Tremblings*. Life and books coalesce and become full of daring sideshows—feats of strength, passionate infinities, throwaway prefaces, the hide and seek of clowns and pseudonyms.

Saturdays: Charades. Living room furniture is pushed back and invited guests join in carnival and farce, romance and heartbreak, grief and salvation.

Sundays: there's praying, resting, recuperation, little discourses or sermons—afternoon walks, taking in the cityscape, the landscape, the churchscape.

Carnival

Fear and Trembling gives us sideshows: a weaning mother mimics a weaning Godhead. Abraham strides about as a whistling shopkeeper. These are highwire acts, difficult realities, impossibilities for assistant professors. Thinking becomes contrapuntal, a fertile mix of the ethical, the poetic, the dialectical—not impersonal, imperial argument or reliable knowledge.

He slips into the garb of a parson, professor, lawyer, editor, journalist, dramatist, bachelor, master thief—a Socratic flaneur, writer *sans portfolio*. It rubs off on me. My file identity as professor is overcome by motorcycle escapades, singing on stage with Leontyne Price (in blackface, no less), peering down from the Golan Heights to the Valley of Tears. Each is a flash of identity. I'm arm in arm with my granddaughter by the Guadalquivir. I'm talking on a St. Olaf lawn.

Think of the circus vitality, the immortality, of his titles: *Either/Or, Prefaces, Repetition,* or the clincher, Kierkegaard's 600-page discourse that goes by the shorthand title, *Postscript.* Spiffed up in full regalia, the full title is *A Final Unscholarly Afterthought, Sequel to Scraps of Philosophy: A Mimicking, Pathos-filled, Dialectical Compendium, an Existential Provocation.* Talk about riot and carnival! Odd creatures like *Prefaces* or *Either/Or* break up literary cubicles. They're Socratic irritants that teach me Socratic ignorance, bafflement, helplessness, joy. Why expect the closure of definitions, the closure of non-circus and un-difficult reality?

I relish his images and quips. His book *Prefaces* is, yes, nothing but prefaces. He says they are "like tuning a guitar, like chatting with a child, like spitting out a window." He calls it the work of "a light-hearted ne'er-do-well." Yet this is a world-famous Christian thinker!

His fetching titles—*A Final Unscholarly Sequel to Scraps of Philosophy*—spark me beyond scholarship. They're carnivalesque. His menageries let *me* be a menagerie—father-professor, wanderer-musician, family-chief-of-staff, seeker-of-home-scape, social butterfly.

Unconcluding finale

Socrates-Kierkegaard passes on the baton of authentic response to me. His elusiveness shows up in the feint and parry of those books—part literature, part philosophy, part polemic, part sermonic, part farce, part who-knows-what. Not all books have a neat and proper place on the shelf. My friends don't fit snugly in a well-labeled social-cultural niche—thank God! Why think it's different for me? There's no single translucent niche tagged with my name.

If I'm only my social and file identities—professor, father, Portland resident, musician—I'm truncated. Happily, my existential bits and pieces let me bloom—in walks with my son, in cheering my granddaughter, in assembling poems, in performing Elgar's *Salud D'amour*. I want to relish each fleeting face in the theater of me—and mourn those I can't relish and want to disown. I want to relish those others who open their circus souls to me in ways that open mine.

Kierkegaard's existential contribution is his actual performing—playing out the paths of pathos and mimicry, dialectic and lyric, making a difficult, shifting reality. The play rubs off on me as I savor and fear my multiplicity. This is a carnival of existential richness, difficult but exuberant, comic more than tragic, well beyond the ken of drab assistant professors of Christian thought. Christian existence is no less exuberant, comic, and carnival.

10
Difficult faith and living well

Kierkegaard is usually taken to focus more on life's paradoxes and anxieties than on what makes for a well-lived life. There's something complacently bourgeois about the concept, "a well-lived life"—a successful career, comfort, good money, close-knit family. But this is exactly the sort of success Kierkegaard spent his time criticizing—not because it is intrinsically flawed, but because it is so often taken to bespeak a *religious* life. Bourgeois success is no mark of faith. It's often a *diversion* from faith. Nevertheless, in Kierkegaard's own terms, "a life well-lived" is compatible with faithful living. To see this, we need to separate *secular* "living well" and *faith-filled* "living well"—a *religious* "success." Kierkegaard lets faith be a tacit presence in a well-lived life. Despite the terrifying visibility of Abraham climbing Mt. Moriah, the knight of faith can be a shopkeeper.[1] Fixating on Moriah, faith and living-well collide, but they needn't.

Faithful living

As we've seen, *Fear and Trembling* offers many sketches of faithful living.[2] A quarter of the way in we find an image of faithful living in the unassuming burgher strolling home from work.[3] He is both faithful and living well. He weathers a simple trial of faith: will his wife have roast lamb ready for dinner? Perhaps not. This is a comic—or absurd—counterpoint to Abraham. Apart from traumatic Moriah cases, faithfully living well means taking what comes one's way with ease, fortitude, and grace. A shopkeeper's return home is an instance of simple faith; weaning mothers are, too. Here the crisis is separating infants from mothers, rather than shopkeepers from roast lamb or fathers from sons. Mothers and burghers can be faithful—*and* tied to a good life. It's striking that Johannes never takes faith to be attached to belief-in-God or creeds. That would open the door to abstract theological discussion: does God exist and is obedience always a good thing? For someone striving for faithful living, these discussion topics don't obtrude.

Difficult reality and the sublime

Faith is a way of living that faces up to inescapable incongruities of life, the clashing push-and-pulls that discomfort us. Cora Diamond refers to this as facing "difficult reality."[4] Her example is gazing at a portrait of young men full of life yet only months from death in battle. One sees both full life and life lost, simultaneously. Abraham's ordeal conveys living through difficult reality. We see both his suffering and his reprieve. The faithful burgher whistling on his way home seems to face no difficulty at all. Perhaps faith provides the assurance and trust to get through routine days as well as horrendous crises.

Confronting difficult, twofold reality, faith will be twofold: an openness to trying circumstances that instill fear and trembling and a poise, trust, and assurance that gets us through. If we are lucky enough to escape monstrous circumstances, faith will be the ease, fortitude, and grace—the openness, poise, trust, that can permeate a largely uneventful life. Living faith underwrites our capacity to take a next step joyfully, confidently, despite fear and trembling. If our shopkeeper is our model, it's compatible with living well.

Faith is both cause and cure of trouble. It epitomizes difficult reality. Openness and clear sightedness make us aware of, and hence vulnerable to, troubles to which others could remain blind. To be open to suffering increases one's quota of personal suffering. Yet as if in recompense, faith's trust and assurance help us weather rough spots or catastrophes, including those brought on by our empathy with others. Faith helps us through difficulties that only faith highlights. It's mixed not only with fear and trembling but also with joy and delight. Johannes de silentio asks, "Isn't it true that those whom God blesses He damns in the same breath?"[5] God is difficult reality.

Faith is not a formulae one can post on cathedral doors or recite before dinner. A knight of faith will have little to say about her or his faith, and those who talk a lot may be of little faith. To point to a creed or answer "I'm Lutheran" won't help. And there are difficulties rendering accurate portraits. Even the cleverest ones always fall short, and we can see why. Faithful living is sublime, and the sublime eludes full representation.

As he pauses with the burgher, Kierkegaard speaks of "finding the sublime in the pedestrian."[6] A sublime scene escapes a painter or poet's attempt at full portrait or description. Mountain storms deliver shimmering excess, an overflow of energy that is larger and wider than any depiction. The storm is both depicted and exceeds depiction.

Attempts to represent the sublime are attempts to represent the unrepresentable. The instances of sublimity cited by Kant and Burke are starry heavens, raging seas, or precipitous mountain cliffs. Abraham's trudge, knife in hand, God looming over it all, exemplify such grandiose sublime. A faithful nursing mother with her baby's soft coo, or a shopkeeper anticipating roast lamb and green peas, exemplifies the petite or pedestrian sublime.[7]

Whether grandiose (as on Moriah) or petite (as with a burger or weaning mother), vectors are at cross-purposes: moral terror runs counter to gripping fascination. Abraham may lose his child, the mother may lose the trust of her infant, the shopkeeper may find roast lamb isn't there, perhaps his wife will be absent, too. We're fearful and fascinated. The *petite* sublime is in the everyday—not high in the heavens or in raging seas.

It's a mistake to model faith only on melodramatic outward heroics, as on Moriah. When faith is the wonder of nursing mothers or burghers striding home, fear is downsized, and disquietude, only minor. The mother, the "shopkeeper," and Abraham, provide three improvisations of faith. Each exemplifies trusting openness. Yet what do we make of their differences? Can faith live equally on Moriah, in weanings, and on homeward strolls?[8]

Uncertainty also surrounds the worry about who authors these sketches. If it's de silentio, why trust a writer whose code name is "silence," who sings loudly about silence, and confides he can't understand Abraham? Maybe he writes slapstick parodies of faith—as weanings, as awaiting roast lamb, as an Abraham shrieking to Isaac that he's a madman.

Unstable and contingent

The text lacks a stable figure of faith, a stable author, and a stable register, style, genre, or tonality. It seems up to chance what figure, author, or style we settle in with. Style, tonality, and genre set the aims and moods of writing. Lyric is one mode, dialectic, another; yet we're told that *Fear and Trembling* is a "Dialectical Lyric." We also have burlesque, fairy tale, and fable; satire, farce, and tragedy; the grotesque and the sublime (both petite and grandiose); we have the antinomian, apophatic, and eucatastrophic (a tale with an unexpected finish that's marvelously good[9]). There are scenes that approach slapstick: Johannes mentions that Abraham could skip the bother of a climb—Isaac could simply be killed at home; a parishioner might run from the sermon, knife in hand, to sacrifice his son; the burgher stops to watch rats scamper; his wife serves him lamb. There are the four mothers, each accompanying an Abraham portrait. Is this Tragedy? Comedy? Farce? Is Abraham holding a knife *really* akin to a mother blackening her breast? How can these unstable divertimenti illuminate faith?

The Preface doesn't prepare us for killing scenarios, and the opening "Attunement" (meant to set a mood for thinking) lets us mull wistfully or daydream.¹⁰ That's neither philosophy nor theology. There's a tone of fantasy and "what if" afoot: what *if* we take Abraham (or the nursing mother) to be a figure of faith? *Fear and Trembling* gets rolling as if it's a fairy tale: "Once there was a man who recalled ... " And the *fairy tale* is about a man who had a *daydream*, who remembered "*a beautiful childhood tale.*" This is decidedly *not* a tonality for portraying child sacrifice. And there's nothing dreamy, nostalgic, or beautiful about the trek to Moriah. Is Johannes fanciful? How can fancy unveil reality?

The monstrous Abraham could be a *diversion* from truth. A knife can blind, after all. Chagall's dreamy version of the sacrifice contrasts radically with Caravaggio's hyper-realistic rendering.¹¹ Chagall has Abraham almost whimsically floating among stars, angels, and lambs, unattached to the earth. Perhaps Johannes de silentio inhabits a similar mood (sometimes).

Improvisation and fantasy reinforce Kierkegaard's aversion to doctrinal disputation. Look at the titles of the two books taken as the core of his philosophy: *Philosophical Fragments* and *Unscientific Postscript*. These are shorthand tags. *Fragments*, in full regalia, is *Philosophical Crumbs, or Scraps of Philosophy*. Its follow up, as we've seen, is a 600-page appendix to the diminutive *Fragments*.¹² Is this scholarship, technical philosophy, theology? Perhaps it's kitsch, a joke, or sustained irony.

Let's say *Fear and Trembling* is a text of diverse and indeterminate tonal register, of diverse genres and authorship, and offers a mixed bag of faith's near-exemplars. If so, how can it be a reliable guide? Well, we're shown over and over what faith is *not*. This clears the board for what faith *might be*. Second, by rummaging through candidates that turn out not to pass muster, we get habituated precisely to the *difficulty* of faith—tracking it, living it, through trial and error. Third, there's the positive theme: faith is taking what comes one's way with ease, fortitude, and grace. In another formulation, it's a trusting openness modulated as giving up (or resignation) of power over contingent loss, and then, getting back the world, or love, or faith as a gift. Seeing open trust permeate the comportment of Abraham, the mother, or the burgher, lets us see how faith might permeate any number of lives, including our own.[13] Through de silentio's knack of tracking faith's varied embodiments—in women sewing, in mothers weaning their infants, in shopkeepers—we are led to follow the dispersion of faith through any number of persons of varying circumstances. And we avoid identifying faith with creedal confession. A knack for following the text becomes a knack for seeing faith outside the text. It's a knack for *embodying* trust and openness in living through life's ambiguities.

Underworld and rebirth

Fear and Trembling is a motley or medley stitched loosely together, scene after scene. It's a carnival and horror show and a Chagall-like dreamy sort of art.[14] Abraham first appears in "a beautiful dream" of an old man remembering a childhood story. Giving up waking life for a dream—and then getting waking life back, dream included—is entering the giving up and getting back of faith. Enigmas bear fruit. "Only one who descends to the underworld saves the loved one."[15] Here is a related enigma: "[The one] who works will give birth to his own father."[16] Acknowledging my mother and father is spiritual labor. The complexity of faith becomes the complexity of fixing, establishing, one's rich paternity, and hence, one's birth—and *rebirth*! One goes down into the dark to come up reborn. Such is the uncanny power of imaginative transformations. If we are beings toward death, as Heidegger learns from Kierkegaard, we are equally beings from birth—as Hannah Arendt learns from Kierkegaard.

Levinas sees only the monstrosity of Moriah with its apparent invitation to killing. He misses these quiet images of faith as motherhood, as natality or birth, faith as a tender attention to, and acceptance of, life: faith as watching rats scamper under gutter planks. The denial of the maternal in philosophical thinking is pervasive. A colleague puts it this way: "As philosophers, we have engaged in self-deception in order not to 'messy' the waters of philosophical investigation by recognizing the voice of the maternal. Doing so would complicate an otherwise tidy, 'single-vision' view of the world." She adds, "Leaving out the maternal closes off a morally essential reality."[17] I return to this in my next chapters.

In addition to natality, de silentio's writing provides numerous other glancing perspectives: a critique of bourgeois market society (*Preface*); a critique of direct communication (*Epigraph*); a critique of religion as bible-based hero-worship (*Speech in Praise of Abraham*); an attack on rule-based and bureaucratic conventional morality (*Problema*); an appreciation of domesticity (mothers weaning, shopkeepers strolling home for dinner, a woman sewing). In addition, the little tome provides a slightly pornographic peephole into dream-like blood-and-violence. It provides a range of polyphony (the voice of terror, of praise, of detached analysis), and an array of variations on a theme: Abraham might have dallied, rushed up Moriah, stabbed *himself*, asked *God* to do it, refused outright, done it in despair, or in deception. All this occurs in a little non-book by a non-author.

Final thoughts

Don Quixote can belong in this troop of knights of faith.[18] The mad knight might be the original "Knight of Faith." Quixote was living Christianly and erratically in a world that took him to be mad; yet he was more Christian than they. The merchant-like knight is living Christianly but not erratically, not madly; yet he is more Christian than they. How? He refuses the ethics of convention that *guarantees* that a wife shall not leave her husband without dinner. He will be free of resentment should the meal not be there; he'll feel perfectly at ease. There is a notable delight and a freedom from presumption or moralism. He shows delightful assurance paired with cognitive, moral, and spiritual humility. Though in externals the opposite of Quixote, this sane fellow is also quixotic.

The poet Yehuda Amichai may have faith in mind in his title *Open Closed Open*.[19] Abraham opens to God, closes down in fright, hand closed on the knife. He then opens to a transformed world as the angel speaks. The nursing mother opens her breast to her infant, closes it off in blackening the breast—then opens the infant to a new, more independent world. The shop man opens to the world, imagining even a roast head of lamb awaiting him at home. He finds that possibility perhaps closed—then gets his world back, as fresh as before. Job is wonderfully open, then horribly closed in his anger and grief—then opened by the Whirlwind's gift of new worlds. Faith is giving up Isaac and getting him back.[20]

We started with the question whether faith is compatible with a well-lived life. Focusing on Abraham, the chances seem slim, though if we interpret his trial as a variation on the trial of a weaning mother or a bourgeois shopkeeper, the chances seem good. There's something complacently bourgeois about the concept, "a well-lived life"—a successful career, comfort, good money, close-knit family. But neither a shopkeeper nor a weaning mother are necessarily complacent, free of trials. So the good life, even bourgeois success, can hide in its recesses the necessary trials of Kierkegaardian faith.

11
Faith can't be self-deceptive

Self-deception is defense against threats to moral self-image or integrity. Faithful living is an antidote to self-deception. But how does it work? You might lie to a thief to protect your daughter. That would be deception, but not *self*-deception. To protect yourself, you might lie to your friends, but if you know you're doing this it's not self-deception. In self-deception, I *hide* my lying from myself. I need to hide from myself the facts that threaten my moral self-image. As Melville has it, "When a man suspects any wrong, it sometimes happens that if he be already involved in the matter, he insensibly strives to cover up his suspicions even from himself."[1] Like hiding dirt under the rug, self-deception depletes my goodness and integrity. On the other hand, in proper faith, I hide nothing from myself, making self-deception impossible. My moral self-image is transparent, blemishes and all. Self-deception *prevents* me from facing my moral weakness while faith gives me strength in the face of weakness.

Dynamics

Self-deception has two vectors. There is the deception I direct at others—*I just don't want them to know* I'm a thief. I lie to them. In *self*-deception, I also lie to *myself*. I hide from myself my thievery. I'm ashamed of it; it tarnishes my self-esteem. And I skillfully hide from myself that tarnishing fact. This is easy to spot in children. They lie about stealing a cookie and come to believe in their own lie, protesting their innocence more and more adamantly. They can utterly convince themselves they really *didn't* steal. Adults shake their heads. They know their child is *utterly convinced* of their innocence and will burst into tears if that innocence is challenged. The protest of innocence can gather hysterical momentum.

What are the mechanics? If I skillfully hide a blemished self-image, I must *know what I'm doing* to execute the lie so skillfully. But I'm not *explicitly aware* of what I'm doing. Deep in conversation with you, I skillfully brake for the red light. I'm *explicitly aware* of what I'm saying to you. But my awareness of braking is only *implicit*, not something present to consciousness. The mechanism of self-protection—hiding from myself my thievery—can be as hidden from my *explicit* awareness as braking while conversing. A self-deceiver hides something without being *explicitly* aware of doing so.[2]

My daughter has been lying about doing her schoolwork, and I know this. Her teacher asks me why her lessons haven't been turned in. Protecting myself and my daughter, I blurt out, "But she *has* done her homework and has passed it in! You must have mislaid it!" I might not be self-aware that I'm lying. I want desperately to preserve my self-image as a good father with a good daughter. I blurt out that my daughter is blameless with no more awareness that I'm *hiding* something than my unawareness in an emergency that I'm braking when I screech to a halt. I'm smoothly skillful in hiding tarnishing facts about my daughter from myself, and smoothly skillful in hiding from myself the brute fact that I'm skillfully hiding those facts.

It's commonplace to skillfully do things without self-awareness. I correct my imbalance as I'm about to slip on ice—yet I don't know what exactly goes into the performance. I know how to correct my psychic imbalance when something threatens to wound my self-image—say the painful revelation that

I don't monitor my daughter's homework adequately. Children of five or six can be enormously skillful in evading damage to their self-image—"Mom, I didn't steal the cookies!" Self-deception is a kind of "learned instinct" as automatic and "preconscious" as catching one's balance on ice. When we "slip up" in maintaining a moral balance we can correct ourselves through explicit apologies. Or we can regress to the hidden strategy of cover-up.

Transparency

Faith makes self-deception impossible. As we've seen in the last chapter, Kierkegaardian faith is living past despair, transparently, hiding nothing from yourself in circumstances that threaten your sense of moral viability. Being of faith is acknowledging who you are and your position, with full knowledge that unexpected, inescapable contingency could destroy the self you now are. Imagine *Fear and Trembling*'s weaning mother—*without* faith. Even as she blackens her breast, she tells herself that her infant "won't notice a thing." A tremor in her hand betrays the contrary. A friend tactfully asks about her trembling. She hides the truth from herself, blaming caffeine. Faith would acknowledge that despite her best intentions, her infant might be harmed. She lacks this faith. Her body shows fear and trembling not simply because of objective circumstance but because she is in the risky project of lying to herself in self-defense. Living faithfully would acknowledge uncertainty and contingency.

To protect my investments in power and efficacy, I may come to deny any uncertainty or fragility that render me powerless. I bury this denial from myself in a preconscious reflex akin to my preconscious braking. The (hidden) motivation is to shore up things I control and deny vulnerability. To relentlessly assert prerogatives of the mastering, executive self strips the world of the background against which *humane* response shimmers. We want to believe that to understand is to master. Johannes admits he cannot understand Abraham, the knight of faith. That's a *good* thing to admit. The knight is not an object to be studied but a marvel to behold. Marvels surpass and silence the will to mastery.

Foregoing mastery

The faithful nursing mother is not self-centeredly wrestling with a problem, gathering her resources to master it. The world presents tasks: the child must be weaned, set free. The faithful mother will realize that how the weaning goes is not totally in her control. If she is of faith, she awaits her time, the child's time, and doesn't cast blame if her timing or manner is off. We remember the "shop man knight of faith" jauntily returning home expecting that his good wife has a meal waiting. He realizes, we surmise, that how his dinner goes is not totally in his control. He awaits his time and will accept the world come what may. The table is set or not. The evening meal is present (or absent). Both nursing mother and strolling burgher listen willingly, patiently to an outer, intimate world. Those of little faith try to wrestle the world to submission, to make it answer their needs and aspirations.[3]

When I turn to technique to skirt or subvert obstacles that confront me, I become, for the moment, a technocrat, a tool-wielder, not a person of faith. Yet we are existentially susceptible to love, death, grief, shame, or birth. These are matters that can't be diminished or enhanced by techniques I might wield, or by tools others might offer me. If I'm offered a technique—"Don't cry, take a walk, you'll get over it" or "Trust in the Lord, don't probe—answers are at hand!" or "Grow up!" I'd be correct in rejecting these offers. Psychological, doctrinal, rabbinical, or ministerial nostrums seem to be tools to lean on and apply. But these are often little more than superficial and condescending diversions.

Death, love, and grief are not problems to solve with appropriate tools, nor will knowing more about them help. Knowing more about delights (in love) or aches (in grief, death, or love) only deepens our appreciation of their elusiveness, their bottomless mystery—veiled and shifting, alluring and repelling. Enigmas don't retreat but expand and fan out as we undergo grief, innocent delight, vulnerability, or love.

Philosophers are trained to attack and subdue the ambiguous and problematic. They take offence at those regions where faith is at home. Commitments to rational progress, whether Hegelian, Analytic, or Marxist, aim to disenfranchise pervasive darkness. We aim to subdue. But ultimate vulnerability and contingency disarm us. Simone Weil calls the contingencies that are disturbing, harmful, painful, "affliction." She writes:

> To acknowledge affliction means saying to oneself: "I may lose at any moment, through the play of circumstances over which I have no control, anything whatsoever I possess, including those things which are so intimately mine that I consider them as being myself."[4]

Stanley Cavell says the loss of self might be a condition of gaining a self. As he puts it, "[The] possessing of a self is not—is the reverse of—possessive; ... it is the exercise not of power but of reception."[5] Faith, then, is the vulnerable condition under which a self is transparently received, with full knowledge that at any moment it might be taken.

Faith is first a trusting openness or transparency. It can now be further specified as *a giving up* (as in Job or Abraham or a weaning mother) and *a getting back*, a receptivity to a return of the world, return of the son, return of the nursing infant. Giving up and getting back is the double movement of faith in *Fear and Trembling*. Self-deception is willfully, strategically, trying to engineer a clean bill of moral health, which means willfully dismissing the verdicts of our own experience.

We cannot willfully take possession of the self we aim to be. To avoid self-deception and abide in faith is to remain open to the world despite the contrary desire to master it—to close in on it, take possession of it. Affliction, our condition, speaks only to a less than lordly self, only to a soul. Faith is at risk from several corners, not least our fear of the evident fragility of life. Love and faith reside amidst vulnerability to contingency. Love and faith are undergone enigmatically, without rules for when to hold and when to let go—when to relinquish, when to welcome.

Distorting simplicity

Self-deception is often a futile attempt to simplify and violently purify our virtue—for example, to deny that we or those we care about are flawed. Faith, in contrast, is a subtle twofold (or multifold) relinquishment of will-to-power, a willingness to await reception, and a ready responsiveness to what may be given. Faith is a giving up and getting back that sustains without simplification what emerges as a veiled and vulnerable complication and expansion of virtue in a difficult reality.

A narrowing of virtue can kill. Single vision is subject to "hypo-nomia," a compulsive adherence to narrow rules—to inflexible norms. It blocks out multivalent circumstance. Kindness can conflict with truth, mercy conflict with justice, strength, with humility, and so on. An expansive virtue such as faith listens to increasing complexity. Kierkegaard links faith to objective uncertainty.

When we simplify in order to preserve a single constricted and violently "purified" virtue, we sacrifice what does not fit. A soldier commits suicide because he can't live up to a categorical and pure demand: because others died for him, he must die for them. His survival profanes the nobility of their sacrifice. A celebrity singer, in her own eyes only a *would-be* beauty, takes her life because she lets her vision of superlative beauty become isolated from all other value, and demands categorically that she be "pure beauty." She excludes herself from being ordinarily beautiful, or simply attractive.[6]

Sometimes a self of constricted vision kills others, sacrificing them as scapegoats in the name of "purifying" the social landscape. The self installs restrictive absolutes: the pure Aryan or Christian, the pure male who despises any hint of heterodox sexuality (it's all brotherhood and guns), the pure female, who must be sexy and striking. Our ideals can slip from legitimacy to poison: "No one's better than anyone else!" "You're mine, my dear!" "Anything less than winning is losing!" "The unexamined life is not worth living!"

A colleague asks, "Couldn't faith's 'I hide nothing from myself' be denatured into a ... remorseless, light-glaring-in-the-face interrogation of the self, distorted and distorting?" He adds:

> It strikes me that living by faith ... is so to live that faithfulness itself is rarely dwelt upon and certainly does not become overtly programmatic in the faithful person's life. Faith-fullness is an unforced, active, inward and sympathetic attention to what is uncertain and contingent, even while it is acknowledged to be uncertain and contingent. But it is not, or not often, attentive to itself. Perhaps this is, phenomenologically, part of the experience of faith as a gift, a theological (and not a cardinal) virtue.[7]

I find this very helpful.

If self-deception *closes off* morally essential realities, faith *opens* to them— ever more opens to ever more of them. It is the opposite of embracing a dogma. Love, too, opens endlessly, shifting between relinquishment and embrace. I'll stand by the equation: what goes for faith goes for love. And what goes for Kierkegaardian faith is the ultimate impossibility, of anything like self-deception. Whether mortals can attain or receive such utter faithfulness, and what the odds are, is quite another matter.

Faith enables

Can Abraham simultaneously believe that it's wrong to sacrifice his child yet believe that it's right to obey God? The issue may be less about belief than about conflicting trusts, trusting ethics and trusting God, when these trusts collide. If Abraham suffers a collision of trusts, the question is how he weathers that collision, how he proceeds without betraying one trust or the other, how he maintains openness and poise in a situation that is catastrophic. Can this particular person, Abraham, weather this conflict—can he emerge unbroken? Can Abraham emerge with love of the world rather than hatred or despair of it? Love and trust are neither propositional beliefs nor creeds. They require a readiness to accept gifts bestowed and withheld. They underwrite his poise in the face of an unspeakable reality.

Keeping faith is compatible with being quite agnostic about what propositions might ground one's achieved and ever-renewed assurance or poise. The conduct of life is rooted in primitive assurances as much as foundational tenets. At some point reasons for what we do run out. We discover and affirm what we love, where we abide, what moves us.[8] When reasons run out, we can slip into despair and skepticism—or abide in trust that we can nevertheless go on, and the world will be somehow still with us. Of course, a faith may be ill advised, foolish, infantile, or self-destructive. But a stance doesn't fail the way an assertion does. A person does not fall apart or regain poise the way propositions do. My stance is present in my living with poise and openness—or not. Snow is here to grace the limbs of my trees—or not. I don't attempt to ground my faith any more than I attempt to ground the grace and illuminations of snow.

Faithful living is a life better lived. An undeceived life is an improvement over a self-deceived one, and a life of trust and openness is better than a life of mistrust and refusal. A willingness to undergo the giving up and getting back of faith leaves one accessible to rebirth. This must be a boon to hopes for a life well lived. Faithful living stays open to marvels.[9]

12
Nurturing love

Death is a grim reaper; birth, a seedling, full of hope. Birth is the promise of beginnings and fresh starts; death, news that there are no more beginnings or fresh starts.

Death is familiar philosophical fodder. But why do finales overshadow brave openings and beginnings? Why are birth, hope, and new growth so seldom explored philosophically? It's as if we take Silenus's bitter warning to heart, "Better to die young, best never to have been born."[1] Then there's Job's aching misogyny: "Man who is born of a woman is of few days and full of sorrow: he cometh forth like a flower and is cut down."[2] Should he have been born of an angel, a demon, of God—or (heaven forbid!) of a man?

Mortality, natality

Talk of birth and beginnings is talk of women, wombs, and nursing—apparently unfit topics for philosophical discussion (until very recently).[3] Kierkegaard is the exception here, giving prominence to mothers, birthing, and weaning. Hannah Arendt holds that the condition of natality—being born—is a limit-condition of life just as momentous as mortality.[6] While the prospect of death can revitalize on-going projects, meditation on birth can lead to the intimate wonder that I exist—in this body, in this age, in this language, held and released by this mother.[7]

Giving birth is woman's provenance; giving death is man's. Abraham raising a knife against his son portends violence and death, yet birth and nurturance are no less prominent in *Fear and Trembling*. Johannes de silentio sings of four mothers and four infants. These might be cameo appearances of Isaac's weaning from Sarah, or of Abraham's weaning from God. (God might blacken his breast so that Abraham will be weaned from the presumption he will always be cradled by the Divine.) As we've seen earlier, the mother–child motif counterbalances the four father-sons on Moriah. An infant's love can blossom as more than hunger at weaning, and a mother's love can blossom as more than feeding. An impending weaning can be a midrash on, an interpretative reading of, an impending bloody sacrifice. Or an impending sacrifice can be an interpretative reading of impending weaning.

The biblical Ur-text, as Kierkegaard presents it, remains always elusive. Abraham mounting Moriah carries colliding imperatives: "Protect thy son!" "Do not kill!" "Sacrifice thy son!" Johannes can't unravel the enigmas. Faith remains a marvel, the marvel of weathering trials of intimacy and separation, closeness and distance. There are other issues raised.[4] We may be baffled by faith—by the source of its uncanny strength—and amazed that faith can be gendered. It's embodied in a father who promises death, separation from life, despite his hope for Isaac's return. Simultaneously, it's embodied in a mother who promises release into life, despite the loss of her suckling.

Scandalous omission

The challenge of interpreting the binding of Isaac (the Akedah) is as old as its first telling. Today it is immediately taken as scandal. A secondary scandal is that scholars of *Fear and Trembling* have said next to nothing (until very recently) about weaning—Kierkegaard's brilliant intervention in the discussion.

Sarah's exclusion from the drama is sometimes noted, but few have noticed the inclusion of weaning mothers. How could the mothers be missed? Perhaps the horror of Abraham's knife is blinding. Perhaps the sight of weaning and blackened breasts is unsavory. Mother-infants create two levels of disruption. The first is their bare presence *at all*—anywhere. The second is juxtaposing weaning and child sacrifice. Why put potential violent paternal child sacrifice in proximity to tender maternal weaning?

A father's near-sacrifice of his son is a measure of faith's raw intensity. By osmosis the intensity of a maternal weaning is inflated: horror leaks down to the mothers. In a reverse motion, a mother's compassion—a measure of faith's nurturance—dilutes the intensity of Moriah. Tenderness rises up to the mountain. The upshot is not that the trudge to Moriah is as banal as breastfeeding, or that the weaning is as horrific as child sacrifice. The lesson is that our understandings are labile, in motion, like swinging emotions and morphing facts.

Grappling with the enigmas of faith is improvisational and eludes the philosopher's search for sure-grip conclusions. De silentio leaves the exact level of horror, tenderness, or momentousness undecided. Faithfulness can be horrific or as tender, or pedestrian, as a shopkeeper strolling across town.[5] There's yet another disturbing possibility: what if de silentio's obsession with Moriah is no more than the thrill of having a ring-side seat at a blood-curdling faux-religious carnival sideshow? Faith is of infinite existential concern. But if silentio is only a curious or astounded or prurient onlooker—then all we get is gawking, or merely a dialectical knot for intellectual amusement.

Avoiding the maternal

There's an avoidance of philosophical and literary attention to birth, of being brought into life, of growing into youth and attaining independence.

There's inattention to the phases of life under maternal nurture and tutelage.[6] Attention to death, in contrast, is ubiquitous in literature and philosophy. Tolstoy is one of the first to depict screams of childbirth, and to expose a father's agony in hearing it.[7] Males are depicted as—and in fact *are*—powerful in public space: in politics, war, conquest, and conflict. Family life, especially the rearing of children, is in "private space." A secluded room seems to be the place for women's effectuality. Novels of family life flourish from Jane Austen on, but even here, accounts of early nurturing are incomplete. The Odyssey, bucking a pattern, introduces home life and opens with a mother bidding her son farewell as he wends from adolescence into maturity. His infancy is cited through the person of the nurse who bathed him, and thus knows his scar. Apart from Rousseau's *Emile*, philosophers write little about family or childhood until mid-twentieth-century feminism. Readers of *Fear and Trembling* to the present day overlook the appearance of mothers. Through 320 pages of *Feminist Interpretations of Søren Kierkegaard (1997)*, mothers are not mentioned once.[8] It's as if motherhood, giving birth, and weaning, are risqué, or dangerous to linger with. There's no such hesitation in dealing with death.

Lyric and dialectic

The text is carnivalesque, moving from motherly knights of faith to Abrahamic ones, from knights of infinite resignation to tales of Agnes and the Merman, from strolling shopkeepers to Socrates' advice. Poetry, lyric, keeps the carnival in motion. *Fear and Trembling* is subtitled a lyrical dialectic. The first two-fifths feature lyrical openings, experiments in how to begin thinking of faith. The remaining three-fifths contain intermittently dialectical sections. It starts with a brain-teaser: "Can there be a Teleological Suspension of the Ethical?" Philosophers favor the dialectical sections; few get immersed in the lyrical openings.

It is as if dialectical conundrums are serious while anything lyric is only poetic fluff. Fairy tales are for mothers to read to kids; philosophers have more serious business. Johannes favors lyric. He begins "Attunement" in a fairy tale mood: "Once there was a man ..." Romantic male poets are often characterized as feminine—as if mature masculine thinkers can't be bothered by images, parables, and lyrical excursions. It's assumed we think only in propositions, never in pictures, parables, Midrashim, or ironic interjections.[9] Kafka knew better. He modeled his "Abraham Parable" on the early "Attunement" parables.[10] A vast secondary literature focuses on the dialectical question of the teleological suspension of ethics. Next to none focus on de silentio's lyricism.[11]

In Hannay's translation, the lyrical beginning sections are titled "Attunement," "Praising Speech," and "Preamble from the Heart."[12] Each starts afresh, in a different mood—as if restarts are demanded. Perhaps initial attempts fail, or failed attempts are the best we can do, or multiple angles are required. Perhaps we must forego the luxury of a single, stable reading. Everything morphs, dizzyingly. These resets suggest that existential questioning outstrips ordinary cognitive capacities. We suffer false starts and are forced to improvise new ones. There are no puzzle pieces awaiting orderly assembly.[13]

Surviving an existential crisis is less a matter of finding a univocal answer than of minimizing painful residues—all the while acknowledging that residues are inevitable. We live with an eternal absence of any single correct reading of pieces of life.[14] One must have courage to move on despite this harrowing absence of solutions. Faith or courage assists taking the next step despite inescapable cognitive gaps.

Silentio's variety of incomplete yet promising introductions is a stark reminder that we don't know the meaning of that trip and may never know it. The rough places are not made plain. Paradoxically, intervention can instigate a new ordeal if tomorrow divinity asks for sacrifice again, endlessly making trouble. Could there be monthly trudges up Moriah? Our lives are never fully plotted. When restarts of the trip to Moriah are linked to mother–infant images, the incomplete plotting is doubled and tripled.[15]

"*Fear and Trembling* will make my name immortal," Kierkegaard crows.[16] He banks on his ingenuity in bringing out the full scandal and spectacle of the Moriah affair. He banks, too, on his dialectical finesse in causing the religious and the ethical to totter in precarious disharmony.[17] And he might well have banked also on the electric coupling of mother–infant to father–son, bringing the maternal center stage, mingling birth with death.

Improvisations

The series of weaning mothers whisper that it is *her* trial at issue, as if mothers are candidate knights of faith. And perhaps they whisper that Abraham is weaning Isaac (not killing him). And perhaps God is weaning Abraham (not destroying him). Then the primal drama becomes the ordeal of love and separation that Gillian Rose depicts.

> If the Lover retires too far, the light of love is extinguished and the Beloved dies; if the Lover approaches too near the Beloved, she is effaced by the love and ceases to have an independent existence. The Lovers must leave a distance, a boundary, for love: then they approach and retire so that love may suspire. This may be heard as the economics of Eros; but it may also be taken as the infinite passion of faith. [18]

To achieve independence in relationship is the exacting project of Kierkegaardian selfhood. If this is correct, we have a two-track story of individuation.

> When the child is to be weaned the mother blackens her breast, for it would be a shame were the breast to look pleasing when the child is not to have it.

> So the child believes that the breast has changed but the mother is the same, her look [is] loving and tender as ever. Lucky the one that needed no more terrible means to wean the child![19]

The mother deceives the child—her breast isn't really black, she makes it black. She isn't really rejecting him. These deceptions echo Abraham's pretending that he is insane, pretending that he wants Isaac dead.[20] Later, toward the end of *Fear and Trembling*, the merman, facing Agnes, will also plunge into pretense and deception. Kierkegaard is fascinated with the regions between ethical, religious, and aesthetic life-spheres, where distinct guidelines—for instance, "never deceive," "always obey God"—break down.

Is Abraham Godly—or a Madman? For Isaac, and many others, probably both. In an early version of events, Abraham presents himself as a madman. The mother is more discrete. She shows her face as a remembrance of love. The infant is neither swallowed by the mother's presence nor abandoned by the mother's absence.

The second mother presents a less successful attempt at weaning.

> When the child has grown and is to be weaned the mother virginally covers her breast, so the child no more has a mother. Lucky the child that lost its mother in no other way![21]

Here is the third telling:

> When the child is to be weaned the mother too is not without sorrow, that she and the child grow more and more apart; that the child which first lay beneath her heart, yet later rested at her breast, should no longer be so close. Thus, together they suffer this brief sorrow. Lucky the one who kept the child so close and had no need to sorrow more![22]

Both mother and child suffer separation, but their sorrow is brief. Brief, because mutual? Their separation does not require concealment, in contrast to versions one and two. Shared grief enables them to sustain a more promising relationship.

The fourth and last version has Abraham drawing the knife, but with a shaking hand: seeing this, "Isaac had lost his faith." Lost faith in God, or in his father?

The four miniature retellings, when paired with four weaning mothers, reenact reopenings to life, release into life. This is the telos of nursing, weaning, and maternal care. Life ends in death and begins with birth and rebirth. The lessons of openings to life and the harsh separations of death are inconclusive. Perhaps separation and closeness in love, whether between mother and child or father and child, or both before God, can be tentatively explored but not helpfully resolved. Johannes moves on after these lyrical proposals. He becomes largely dialectical. He leaves the full meaning of these scenarios, and of the *Akedah*, in mid-air. We must be weaned from them.

Carnival

The text is carnivalesque. Lyric, poetry, is what keeps the carnival in motion, moving from Abraham to mothers, from knights of resignation to Agnes and the Merman, from strolling shopkeepers to Socrates' advice. Philosophers favor the dialectical sections; few get immersed in the lyrical openings. It is as if dialectical conundrums are serious while lyric is poetic kid's stuff. Fairy tales are for mothers to read to kids; philosophers have more serious business. Johannes begins "Attunement," as we've seen, in a fairy tale mood: "Once there was a man …"

Surviving an existential crisis is less a matter of finding a univocal answer than minimizing painful residues—all the while acknowledging the eternal absence of any single correct reading of a piece of one's life. But readings, even if fairy tales, must be ventured. One must have courage and faith to move on despite this harrowing absence of ready-made solutions.

It's futile to try to get a sense of our lives by peeking in on our death and last days. It's equally futile to get a sense of our lives by peeking in on our birth and early years. Our lives are ambiguous and never fully plotted. They require glances both forward and backward, as ambiguous and incomplete as these must be. De silentio instills this wisdom. When restarts of the trip to Moriah are linked to mother-infant images, the incomplete plottings are doubled and tripled. This does not detract from the impact of the text but sets it shimmeringly alive.[23]

13
Socrates: Of woman born

Plato's *Symposium* explores Eros. *Fear and Trembling* explores faith, and faith is "the highest passion in a human being"[1]—a passion close to love. Maternal love of infants is depicted in *Fear and Trembling*. A swain's unrequited love, and Agnes' love of a Merman are also central motifs.[2] Both Plato's and Kierkegaard's texts are about enigmas of passion and love.

Socrates attends a banquet whose speakers represent a smattering of celebrities. Before the celebrity talks begin, an unnamed flute girl is asked to leave. We'll see why.[3] Aristophanes, the comic poet, gives a hilarious speech on love hardly topped by Socrates' speech. Socrates reports what the mysterious Diotima tells him about love. The speeches are interrupted by the drunken Alcibiades' lovelorn outburst. He has utterly failed to seduce Socrates and is violently offended.

Kierkegaard is an absence behind the voice of Johannes de silentio. Plato is an absence at the banquet table. There is silence about the flute girl's entrance and dismissal. Socrates is bafflingly silent about his *unexamined faith* in Diotima's words. Why does he refuse to question her? And what gall gives *her* permission to interrogate *him*? Why is a woman privy to knowledge of love—and Socrates beholden to her for that knowledge? *The Symposium* is full of riddles.

Agnes and Diotima

The last pages of *Fear and Trembling* feature a woman, Agnes, teaching love. She is the last act, after many earlier attempts to corner love and faith. For Plato, Diotima and Alcibiades are culminating acts. Kierkegaard's Agnes and Plato's Diotima teach love to mature males. They teach hybrid creatures. Socrates is human but half way to divinity and awaits Diotima. The merman is animality half way to humanity and awaits Agnes to humanize him.

Eros first appears for Plato in the figure of a flute girl. Flutes are for light entertainment. They have exceptional powers of arousal. The flute girl gets dismissed so as not to let erotic music contaminate banquet talking—poetic, scientific, and philosophical. Yet the dialogue closes with the return of unbridled Eros—the drunken uproar of Alcibiades. He is "accompanied by the shrieks of some flute-girl they had brought along."[4] Alcibiades alludes to the eroticism of "the greatest flautist" and "the meanest flute-girl" as he rails about his failure to seduce Socrates.

Plato's flute girl raises the possibility—quickly withdrawn—that passionate music might accompany poetry and philosophy. Kierkegaard's Johannes de silentio mixes philosophy and poetry, penning a "lyric dialectic." Although Plato seems to dismiss poetry in *The Republic*, here he slyly allows poetry and philosophy to couple. Agathon (poetry) competes with philosophy (Socrates), and both are judged superior speakers. Socrates' tale of Diotima is literary, theatrical, and poetic. The *Symposium* mixes poetry and rigorous thought throughout.

Will Socrates win the competition of speeches in praise of love? Who will judge? "Dionysus will soon enough be the judge of our claims to wisdom!"[5] Alcibiades-Dionysus enters to crown *both* Socrates and Agathon. Why should philosophy be judged by passion? Plato refuses to let dialectic dominate. Philosophy dances with an erotic and poetic partner.

Hybridity I

Socrates is divine-human while the merman, in *Fear and Trembling*, is fish-human. A hybrid has advantages over a purebred. Animals escape existential crisis by relying on instinct; divinities escape it through exemption from death. For mortals, death creates urgency about life. Having a god on one's shoulder, or instinct in one's gut, mitigates ethical angst. As long as the merman is exclusively fish-of-the-sea, he will act on instinct without worry. As long as Socrates is exclusively inhabiting god's eternity, he'll be securely ethical and without angst. Animals and gods can duck the ethical imperative to know oneself.[6] Alcibiades accuses Socrates of hybridity, of joining a godlike capacity to resist seduction with a very human power to seduce. Socrates and the Merman, one half-divine, the other half-fish, illuminate human complexity by falling partially outside it. Here is Johannes *de silentio* on Agnes' innocent love, and the merman-seducer:

> The merman ... has called out to Agnes, [and] with his smooth talk has coaxed from her, her secret thoughts. She has found in the merman what she was seeking, what she gazed down to find in the depths of the sea. Agnes is willing to follow him down. The merman has taken her into his arms, Agnes twines hers about his neck trustingly and with all her soul she abandons herself to the stronger one. He is already at the sea-edge, bending over the water to dive down with his prey. Then Agnes looks at him again, not fearfully, not questioningly, not proud of her good luck, not intoxicated with desire, but in absolute faith, with absolute humility like the humble flower she deemed herself to be. With absolute confidence she entrusts to him her entire fate. —And look! The ocean roars no more, its wild voice is stilled, nature's passion—which is the merman's strength—deserts him, the sea becomes dead calm ... Then the merman collapses, he is unable to resist the power of innocence, his element becomes unfaithful to him, he

cannot seduce Agnes. He leads her home again, he explains to her that he only wanted to show her how beautiful the sea is when it is calm, and Agnes believes him.[7]

The merman loses Agnes because he is not *pure* sea-monster. He is more than ravishing instinct. He's overcome with her innocence. He is neither pure monster nor pure human:

> The merman is a seducer, but when he has won Agnes's love, he is so moved by it that he wants to belong to her entirely. –But this, you see, he cannot do, since he must initiate her into his whole tragic existence, that he is a monster at certain times, etc., that the church cannot give its blessing to them. He despairs and in his despair plunges to the bottom of the sea.[8]

The merman cannot absorb Agnes' lesson, that love is utter trust, utter openness, faith. He can't wean himself from his animality.

The Agnes story is a continuation of the earlier weaning stories. In one version, a mother tries to wean her infant, to whom she is instinctually attached. But for lack of trust, she fails. She plunges into despair, abandoning the child. The merman tries, but fails, to wean himself from lust. Should Alcibiades try to wean himself from lust for Socrates?

Agnes has faithfulness and innocence. She changes the merman forever. He cannot seduce her and feels guilty for wanting to. Here is the second phase of the love story. The merman can remain demonic, a seducer at heart; or he can repent and resign Agnes. Or, paradoxically, he can repent, have faith, and keep Agnes:

> If he stays hidden and dedicates himself to all the torments of repentance [suffering his guilt but not revealing it], he becomes a demon, and as such is brought to nothing. If he stays hidden but entertains no clever thoughts about being able to extricate Agnes …, he will no doubt find peace but

is lost to the world. If he discloses himself, lets himself be saved through Agnes, then he is the greatest human being I can imagine.[9]

Each of the possibilities has a price, including the last one. Becoming a man means relinquishing the dominance of his animal side. It is Agnes who actually provides the merman with future possibilities. She points the way. He can choose to reveal himself, shed sensuousness, and have faith that she will not be lost.

Dynamics of Hybridity

We have Socrates as god-man, the merman as fish-man, and a mother as mother-child. Hybridity is a tensed dynamic of ontologically disparate parts. A hybrid's melding and morphing is rich because it defeats *static* binaries and hierarchies. Through embodying excess *and* deficiency, the hybrid becomes more abundant than either of its component parts, taken separately, or simply aggregated. This opens wild possibilities for being. One can be a man-god or a man-monster, richer than simple monster, simple man, or simple god. Hybridity opens a liberating dynamic of abundance. The downside is the havoc it plays with expectations. We want something *either* a god *or* a mortal, not both; *either* goat *or* person, not both; *either* mother *or* infant, not both. Hybrids shimmer at the edge of vertigo and incoherence. We want freedom from typecasting, but can we avoid falling into anxiety and dizzying ambiguity? Hybridity marries contrasts or opposites: a marriage of heaven and hell (Blake), or a marriage of reason-emotion, sacred-secular, or living-dead, body-soul. For Plato, Eros melds fullness-and-lack.

Plato casts Socrates as both a satyr and godlike. Kierkegaard becomes Kierkegaard-de silentio, and de silentio becomes an old man remembering a fairy tale.[10] His book is both lyric and dialectic. Odd couplings unglue the stability of singular identities. They tax both imagination and living, for how do we live with goat-men, men-gods, mother-Abrahams?

Hybrids unglue single-core identities. Yet original identity is preserved in morphed hybrid identities. Socrates becomes Socrates-satyr, but he remains Socrates (though now more complex). Alcibiades opens the last great speech in the *Symposium*:

> I'll try to praise Socrates, my friends, but I'll have to use an image. And though he may think I'm trying to make fun of him, I assure you my image is no joke: it aims at the truth. Look at him! Isn't he just like a statue of Silenus? You know the kind of statue I mean; you'll find them in any shop in town. It's a Silenus sitting, his flute or his pipes in his hands, and it's hollow. It's split right down the middle, and inside, full of tiny statues of the gods. Now look at him again! Isn't he also just like the satyr Marsyas?[11]

Socrates is satyr, half man/half animal, and full of gods. This is close to Diotima's description of Eros as half-man, half-god.

> As the son of Poros and Penia, his lot in life is set to be like theirs. In the first place, he is always poor, and he's far from being delicate and beautiful (as ordinary people think he is); instead, he is tough and shriveled and shoeless and homeless, always lying on the dirt without a bed, sleeping at people's doorsteps and in roadsides under the sky, having his mother's nature, always living with Need. But on his father's side he is a schemer after the beautiful and the good; he is brave, impetuous, and intense, an awesome hunter, always weaving snares, resourceful in his pursuit of intelligence, a lover of wisdom through all his life, a genius with enchantments, potions, and clever pleadings.[12]

Eros escapes the simple categories mortal/immortal, human/divine:

He is by nature neither immortal nor mortal. But now he springs to life when he gets his way; now he dies—all in the very same day. Because he is his father's son, however, he keeps coming back to life, but then he finds his way to always slip away, and for this reason Love is never completely without resources, nor is he ever rich. He is in between wisdom and ignorance as well.[13]

Socrates is Eros, mortal/immortal.

Diotima

She is the priestess of love. How is she so well informed? Perhaps she's a theatrical convention, a womanly mask through which Socrates speaks. But why can't Socrates speak directly? Does it take a woman to reveal men to themselves?

Love demands confessing vulnerability. It can be frightening for a tough *man* to speak of this. Perhaps it's not so frightening to hear it from an appreciative woman. Socrates invokes an appreciative woman to teach him and his companions. To be credible, she has to be extraordinary. Her pupil is Socrates, no less. Socrates has her *be* extraordinary. He underscores his esteem by letting her turn the tables on him, quiet him. *She* does the Socratic practice of interrogation. She interrogates *him*—and gets away with it. He becomes the ignorant, star-struck pupil. Here is David Halperin:

> Once we admit the possibility that there may be more to being a woman than not being a man, we are obliged to seek for positive reasons behind Plato's startling decision to introduce a woman into the clannish, masculine society of Agathon's household in order to enlighten a group of articulate pederasts about the mysteries of erotic desire.[14]

Halperin concludes:

> Diotima's gender, then, is not a merely peripheral fact or an accidental circumstance, unconnected to her teaching; it is, apparently, a condition of her discourse, and it is inscribed in what she says.[15]

With an authority no male could muster, she speaks of *giving birth* through the body, and of love as generative, giving birth to the beautiful.[16]

Should a feminist applaud the appearance of a woman strong and wise enough to teach Socrates? Diotima envisages ultimate love as several steps above love of a particular body—a kind of *disembodied* love. Can giving birth to an actual baby be inferior, as Diotima avers, to giving birth to a male's spirit or soul? Consider her audience. Diotima addresses men. As a matter of biology, they will never give birth to actual babies. To work for spiritual birth is the best they can hope for. Johannes de silentio goes further than biology. The faithful will "give birth to their own fathers."[17] Elsewhere, Kierkegaard writes, " ... when the child has rested long enough at the mother's breast it is laid at the father's [breast], and he too nourishes it with his flesh and blood."[18]

Perhaps Diotima appears because males have only a broken knowledge of woman's ways of birthing. They will look toward a mother or woman for understanding what spiritual pregnancy or birth might mean. Socrates recruits Diotima, even when the birth in question is spiritual. Yet having Diotima preside brings on ambivalence. Men both long for women's power and target them in envy. In this maelstrom of emotion, it's a stroke of genius for Plato to invent the hybrid, Socrates-Diotima. Through their love of Socrates, a male audience can imagine giving birth, especially as he morphs into Socrates-wise-priestess. If he lets a woman instruct him, get inside him, then they can let Socrates-Diotima instruct or get inside *them*.

Diotima holds Socrates at bay, removing his sting. No one else is allowed to show up his ignorance, to remove his dialogical sting. He lets himself *be stung* by love—by Diotima and her song in praise of love. Usually professing ignorance, Socrates, now confesses that love is the only thing of which he has knowledge. Diotima crashes the party, breaking the barriers against knowing love. This anticipates the hybridity Johannes de silentio uses to clarify love-and-separation: Abraham is weaning-mother and weaning-mother is Abraham. Here, Socrates is Diotima and Diotima is Socrates.

Love and birth

Wisdom is delivered by the wisest of men—Socrates. But Socrates must be feminized. He becomes a mid-wife. Males learn of generative love—giving birth—through accessing a woman's art. For intimate knowledge of giving birth and nurturing, *Diotima* enters. In like fashion, Abraham merges with a weaning *mother* to absorb the arts of nursing, nurturing, and separation. Rather that defer to the wisdom of mothers, males might just as soon close their ears and stay ignorant. Male philosophers haven't seen these as proper topics of discussion. A lack of birthing power challenges a male's vaunted knowledge and also his aspirations to autonomy and control. He depends on a mother and dependency is a vice, so it's best to put that phase of life aside. And a male will resist the indelicacy of imagining life entering through a birth canal. Such wonders and terrors are best sidelined.

If philosophers desiring clear identities, the fluidity of early growth—from birth to weaning, to infancy—is discomforting. And there is a classic anxiety about impregnation. A would-be autonomous male can ask—no mother can ask this—*Is the infant really mine?* Obsessions with fixed identities rule out fluid, hybrid, and uncertain identities. If all this is roughly true, Plato and Kierkegaard break the mold. They give expression to a female voice tolerating fluidity, and foregoing vaunting power.

Love blossoms in romantic attachment and also in birth and beginnings. It blossoms in a mother's visceral sense of pre-natal connectedness, and in the subsequent separation-yet-connectedness of nursing and weaning. For men, a primal love from and for mothers retreats as identification with fathers increases. A boy must follow the steps of the father. He may feel anger at losing a mother's full attention as she collaborates in a boy's shift toward the father. This shift toward respect for a father can hide an emerging distrust and avoidance of love. Young girls face different complications. They are seldom weaned by a father from a mother's love. Lasting into their teens at least, connection with a mother's love is stronger for them than for boys. In some ways stunted in their knowledge of love, men seek instruction from women.

Socrates needs Diotima to teach him love. Males, to be whole and wise, need a dramatic celebration of femininity-and-procreation. Diotima urges males to become women by giving birth to themselves. The focus here is on generative love rather than Alcibiades' sexual passion. Diotima is a counterweight to an exclusively lusty, this-worldly Eros.

Socrates is sometimes criticized for his abstinence and denigration of the bodily *per se*. But perhaps his chastity is mainly a rebuke of the sexual exhibitionism of Alcibiades. Males need a love that transcends sex, that allows for ambiguities, ambivalences and hybridities. Socrates and his double, Diotima, excite this tolerance of ambiguity. Diotima must "talk like a man," be assertive and self-possessed. Socrates must "listen like a woman," and defer to Diotima. Alcibiades, the manliest of warriors, moans like a woman spurned.

How does Johannes di silentio picture love or faith? There's nothing straightforward about a patriarch ready to sacrifice his son. There's nothing straightforward about the analogy between a father ready to kill his son on the basis of faith and a mother ready to risk harm to her infant as she readies herself to wean him. Abraham is weaned from God, as an infant is weaned from its mother—all the while preserving fluid love. Love models transitions from union-to-separation and from separation-to-union. As Gillian Rose puts it, love retains just enough separateness and togetherness to allow "love to suspire."[19]

Lovers are intensely linked-and-unlinked. Ordinary speech stumbles to convey the chaos of love's reality. Love comes from angels, gods, a Diotima, a madman, perhaps even an Abraham—from a simple mother, an Agnes or a Merman. Love calls on ordinary mortals to become half something else.

Death and birth

We are temporal creatures that die. We are creatures *toward* death. We are also creatures *from* birth. Children, parents, siblings, friends penetrate and animate our lives as in recurrent *rebirth*. The masculine calls us to heroism facing death. The feminine and maternal call us to life, to ever new beginnings. A philosophy that excludes love and becoming, that privileges the finality of death over the wonders of birth, is dismal. In *Symposium*, Socrates does not head an all-male club, for he brings Diotima to the center of the Socratic venture.

Kierkegaard feels the pull of Socratic ignorance, the pull of the maternal in weaning mothers, and the complex romance between Agnes and the merman. Neither Kierkegaard nor Plato think that passions or love only corrupt, nor that philosophy is exclusively orderly, free of Eros. Socrates looks up toward transcendent forms and down toward the body, enjoying an identity part goat, part-divinity, part-human; part-male, part-Diotima. De silentio looks up at horrors on Moriah and looks down at nursing mothers and gives us Agnes in love with the merman. Such tempering, blurring, and sometimes biting improvisations provide a glimpse of what lies beyond Moriah, or beneath its shadow—a landscape more human and humane.[20]

14
Literature, philosophy, and existential contributions

A literary genius and philosopher combined—not to mention a radically religious writer—Kierkegaard is anomalous, disrupting the norms. His work creates a disordered or hybrid status, not just literary, not just philosophical, not just religious, but a bit of all three, precariously poised in Copenhagen. In this, he resembles Socrates the interrogator, precariously poised in Athens—obeying the law yet challenging it, a good citizen yet not a good citizen. Kierkegaard's most philosophical texts—*Postscript* and *Philosophical Crumbs*—seem overtly Socratic, and his pseudonymous literary works, say, *Either/Or* and *Fear and Trembling*, are, too.[1] Socrates intervenes existentially in face-to-face encounters. He stops, stings, and interrogates Athenians, often abandoning them—confused and without answers. Kierkegaard replicates the Socratic sting that gives birth to a soul.

Philosophical poet

Kierkegaard is not a novelist, though "The Diary of the Seducer" reads like one. He's not a dramatist, though *Stages on Life's Way* restages Plato's *Symposium*. He's not an essayist, "man of letters," or journalist. Kierkegaard has been called "a kind of poet" though he doesn't write a single poem.[2] When a field biologist encounters strange plants outside existing taxonomies, she gets to name a new species. We want to get quirky things on the map.

Kierkegaard's work is even self-replicating. *Either/Or* spawns *Stages on Life's Way*. *Crumbs* (or *Fragments*) spawns *Postscript*. The body of work passes on its genes to Ibsen and Kafka, to Rilke, Auden, and Dinesen.[3] Along a different branch of the family, he appears in Ingmar Bergmann, John Updike, and Woody Allen, and sprouts competitors: Heidegger and Wittgenstein, Ortega, and Sartre. He's a riddle like the Mona Lisa—or like the Socrates who smiles and says he knows nothing—even as we know otherwise. We are left smitten but empty-handed.

The Socratic aim is to sidestep "objective knowledge" and to embrace "becoming subjective." This means placing your soul on the line, discerning inner prompts, the tilt of your soul, empty or full. Socrates is a midwife who sees us in labor and assists in new birth. Kierkegaard too would nag, provoke, and push us toward our next self.

Philosophy vs. poetry

Kierkegaard earned the equivalent of a modern PhD, but never became a parson, professor, or lawyer—nor an editor, journalist, or dramatist. He calls himself a "freelancer" when posing as Johannes de silentio in *Fear and Trembling*. But that's just a refusal to be tied down as a dramatist, novelist, poet, or critic. Perhaps he's "a *kind* of poet"—figurative, evocative, allusive, elusive, and enigmatic, as poets often are, and as standard essayists or philosophers *aren't*. He gives imagination and passions plenty of space. On the other hand, he doesn't read like a poet, and doesn't write poems. Modern philosophers have demands of discipline, order, and intelligibility that Kierkegaard ducks. For logical positivists, a poetic philosopher is oxymoronic. Nietzsche's aspiration to be a "music playing Socrates" is just crazy.[4]

On the other hand, Jamie Ferreira embraces Kierkegaard's volatile mix. She cites Robert Frost: "a poetic philosopher or a philosophical poet are my favorite kind of both." And then, cites Wittgenstein: "philosophy ought only to be written as a poetic composition."[5] Poetry can loosen straight-laced philosophy, and philosophy can give structure to poetry. Why not enjoy hybridity?

Misfits

A "book" titled *Prefaces* contains nothing but prefaces. It's not poetry or short story or political polemic. Odd creatures like *Prefaces, Either/Or*, or *Postscript* are full of brilliant writing that explodes cultural cubbyholes. They are Socratic irritants that teach Socratic ignorance. We get baffled, annoyed, helpless—yet captivated. Socrates' companions ask for but are never given adequate definitions. Kierkegaard's books duck genres. But why assume all books have proper places on library shelves? Maybe I expect too much order from the world.

Neither *Prefaces* nor *Either/Or* has a straightforward author.[6] We both do and do not know who authors them. Is *Middlemarch* to be filed under George Eliot or Mary Anne Evans? Evans used a male pseudonym so her work would be taken seriously. Kierkegaard used pseudonyms for less evident reasons. They're not fluffy devices to provoke public interest, nor a way to deflect personal responsibility. They're tools to incite Socratic self-awareness and interpretative alertness.[7] There remain issues of power. Can "Kierkegaard" overrule the claims made by "Climacus," "Johannes de silentio," or "Nicholas Note Bene"? I doubt it.

Try to shelve by genre! You'd consider literature, philosophy, essays, personal meditations—satire, the carnivalesque, polemic. Perhaps Kierkegaard is just entertaining. He says that his *Prefaces* are "like tuning a guitar, like chatting with a child, like spitting out a window."[8] *Fear and Trembling* might be like "tuning a guitar." In fact, an early section is called—exactly—"attunement."[9] Does that help us find a library niche? He calls *Prefaces* the work of "a lighthearted ne'er-do-well."[10] Is there a library shelf for satire and fun?

Is it satire and fun to describe Abraham bringing his son to Mt. Moriah? Why assume that this book is out to *make a case* for Abraham? The first part looks like fables, mood swings, and nightmarish dreams. The second part can become scholastic.[11] Perhaps it's neither essay nor fable nor sermon nor poem nor polemic, but a hybrid dash of each of these. Kierkegaard endlessly invents counter-genres, para-books, unclassifiable publications that question our sense of what forms a piece of writing can take. He gives us the vertiginous sense that there may be no end to such inventiveness—that under his spell, we live and read in infinite possibility.

Kierkegaard calls the Abraham book a "dialectical lyric," which names two of its stylistic features. But it's also an unprecedented invention, a collage of fable, biblical exegesis, social commentary, investigation of "the ethical," "the tragic," and barely concealed farce. It's even burlesque, or what Bakhtin calls "the carnivalesque." If there's a lesson for my soul in all this, perhaps it's that life escapes easy shelving.[12]

Kierkegaard gives us *Prefaces* and *Postscript,* a nearly 600-page tome that dwarfs the slim volume to which it's an appendage, *Philosophical Crumbs, or a Crumb of Philosophy*. What sort of universe have we entered? The full title, as we've seen, utterly dwarfs what shrinks to become *Postscript*. In full regalia, we have *Concluding Unscientific Postscript to Philosophical Crumbs: A Mimic-Pathetic-Dialectic Compilation—an Existential Contribution*. Kierkegaard bends cataloguing expectations to the breaking point. Unfortunately, the shock of the title has ceased to make trouble. We dash on, eager to get to the business at hand: what positions are advanced or attacked, and with what arguments? But an "Existential Contribution" won't have objective *positions* front and center.

Not knowing where Kierkegaard belongs on a disciplinary map raises anxieties, but not our deepest ones. The *Postscript*'s "existential contribution" is to raise our *deepest* need. How can I become sensible of, and shape, my singular life, here and now? Failing to settle matters of genre spins me into existential space, where I slide from worries over literary or philosophical cubicles to worries over whether I've neglected, in my own life, a proper appreciation of my individuality. Have I resisted the pull of the crowd, or the false assurances of careerism and church attendance? The faux-genres he adopts should finally serve freedom and new life, a recovery of soul. *The Concept of Anxiety* tells us that freedom requires passage through "a *sympathetic antipathy* and an antipathetic sympathy."[13] This "Doctor of Dread" has my spiritual health at heart.[14]

Existential contributions

The final tag in *Postscript*'s title is "an Existential Contribution." This is the first time in European philosophy, to my knowledge, that the adjective "existential" is used to point toward personal existence. Kierkegaard addresses readers existentially to elicit life choices. One may be a judge or an aesthete, a shopkeeper or a priest, an uncle, a hero, or a rogue. His genius in its first phase is to give compelling portraits of social ways of being. But that only prefaces a critique of social identities and provocations to the soul. If I'm a parson, I'm made to ask, "Have I, as a parson, lost my soul?"

If Climacus fulfills his promise to provide an "existential contribution," he will have forced me to move from the objective question, "What is it to exist as a soul in love?" to the question, "Am I in love?" A judge may play out his courtroom role, but that's distinct from whether he has his heart in his work, has sold his soul to the devil, or finds anything honorable in the office he holds.

An existential Socratic intervention elicits from *this* judge a self-evaluation. He's startled or unnerved or disquieted by the existential address of another and is then moved to decisively resolve or close down the just-opened field of possibilities. This very judge decides to reform, or resign, or prefer to do nothing—and then cashes out the decision in action (or inaction).

In considering my existence existentially, I focus on what I alone must do to achieve this identity. It's not enough to ask what is generally done in this role. I must forge what that role will be for me uniquely—and then move to secure (however precariously) that identity, my *existential* reality. I leap from a pond's-edge view of what an existential reality requires (say, that I must choose myself, as every human must), to full immersion in another question. Who will I, in particular, be and become? I dive in to settle the matter. Will I rise to the surface (or stay under longer)? With what speed will I move, and to what end? Will I rise to the occasion to do what I must do to be the parson or professor I must be?

Kierkegaard offers me existential space. If I accept, I dive into existential possibilities and then close that openness through decisive resolution and action. He can't complete the process he initiates. He offers possibilities but can't determine which will become mine. A contribution to charity becomes real when it is accepted. Kierkegaard's contribution becomes real when I resolve to accept it. An existential contribution allows me to become who I am by assisting me to become who I will be.[15]

It is hard to underestimate the magnitude of this *Postscript* intention. The comic, dialectic, and tragic are in the service of an infinite demand that can be fulfilled or rejected in any number of ways—no guidelines included. I might be entertained by Climacus' wit, impressed by his dialectical finesse, or moved by the pathos of his descriptions. But his distinctive existential contribution is realized only if I transform myself in light of his offer.

Kierkegaard writes enigmatic unfinished books for the same reason that Socrates engaged in enigmatic, unfinished conversations. The aim is not to advance philosophy or literature as a discipline but to existentially alter its readers and listeners, one by one. Kierkegaard is the Socrates who "makes [those in his presence] ill at ease, and inflicts upon them the unpardonable offense of making them doubt themselves."[16] Kierkegaard writes late in life that his mission has always been Socratic: an installation of self-doubt offered as preliminary to self-transformation.

Existential identity

We can show existential identity formation by reflecting on Henri Bergson's last days.[17] The question he faces in his last days is similar to the question Socrates faces in *his* last days, under trial. Jews in Paris were required to wear yellow armbands after the Nazi takeover. Bergson could have ducked wearing an armband. He was frail and could plead infirmity, staying off the streets. He had been close to converting to Roman Catholicism, which would have undercut his Jewishness. His world renown as a philosopher could have earned him the escape offered to Freud or negotiated by Wittgenstein for his sisters. (The Nazis were not entirely deaf, especially in the late 1930s, to the onus of appearing to be cultural barbarians.)

Yet Bergson, now in his eighties, chose to line up outside in a cold drizzle, wearing the armband marking his identification with the Jews, who were already facing a horror that only grew. He determined his existential identity at that moment, even as his social identity was indeterminate. Was he a Jew, a near Catholic convert, a world-famous intellectual, or just a frail old man too weak to descend to the street? In degrees he was all of these, but social identities didn't determine existential identity. Bergson resolves his life this way and not that.

Kierkegaard's corpus stands to us roughly as Bergson's life does. The corpus can be focused this way or that. We can revel in the choice Bergson made to line up in a cold drizzle. We can revel in Kierkegaard's decision to be Socratic, to pass on an existential task to me.[18] If I exercise only my scholarly resources in search of his cultural or academic niche, his Socratic voice will be silent. He asks me to become myself, not to shelve his books correctly, or to give good scholarly interpretations of them. He enacts Socratic feints and parries, delivering texts that escape my nets—not for the fun of it, but for my greatest good.

The Socratic sting

If I am recipient of an existential contribution, then what I make of the text is up to me: I can throw it aside, be slap dash, or struggle with it. If I decide to struggle, I can be suspicious or resentful or charitable, taking the stance of what Kierkegaard calls "love, that lenient interpreter."[19] If I interpret leniently, with love, I'll be generous and grateful for insights bequeathed. If I interpret suspiciously, as an un-masker, I'll feel false pride, and be grateful for little. If I interpret resentfully, I'll take offense: he's attempted to pull the wool over my eyes. A debunker enjoys domination over the matter at hand.[20]

The debunker can hold that Kierkegaard's oeuvre is a vain attempt to assuage guilt (nothing more), that because of his small stature, his writing is working out a Napoleon complex (nothing more), that his father's sexual guilt made him an emotional cripple. Things are dispraised as masks, not praised for gifts they might bring, and for occasions they might provide for thanksgiving for beauty and worth.

I am a different person depending on the interpretative approach I follow. How much in these texts is a world I can love? How large is the world I must despise or wish dead? What powers my writing? Is it wonder or competitive adrenalin—tender, sympathetic appreciation, or disgust, and resentment? Do I face texts with indifferent royal aplomb? In the broadest sense, reading is an ethical venture that reveals something of what I take to be part of the good life—and, on the other hand, what I take to be beyond the pale. My quickness to find fault with texts can be a stain on my character just as my quickness to find fault with persons can be. I expose who I am existentially in "the what" and "the how" of my reading and writing.

Final thoughts

Socrates hopes his life and connection to truth can have a saving effect on his interlocutors. Kelly Jolley writes, "[Philosophy] does not exist [for Socrates] as a sort of idol of which [Socrates] would be the guardian and which he must defend. It exists rather in its living relevance to the Athenians."[21] Just so, the literature Kierkegaard bequeaths does not live on as a tribute to "the literary life" or as a gift to "the great tradition" of literature or philosophy. These are not temples in which he wished to enshrine his texts and himself. His words exist in their "living relevance" to single individuals in whose souls they lodge as provocation, judge, and inspiration. He writes in veins that are in turn literary or aesthetic, ethical or philosophical, religious or counter-religious, and writes to bring these into conflict and repose. But these veins are not ultimate categories of exploration or veneration for him.

Kierkegaard starts for each reader a trial of self-knowledge, self-resolution, self-realization, and selflessness. (It both is and is not, "all about me"). He conducts trials of existence, where his subjectivity meets mine around love and responsibility, urgency, delight, and suffering. Or in an unexpected image, it's an invitation to sweep onto the floor for a solo dance before God—before such presence as can be pleased or displeased with the tilt of my soul. Kierkegaard brings me to the dance, and perhaps demonstrates some steps, but the rest is up to me. His writing is in my service. In its poetry and philosophy, its comic mimicry and tearful pathos, it's a great gift—an existential contribution.[22]

Epilogue: Truths in the trenches

In poetry, which is all fable,
truth still is the perfection.
—SHAFTESBURY

Witness

Wittgenstein responded to the outbreak of the First World War by joining the Austrian Army as an artillery corpsman. Twenty years later he abandoned teaching at Cambridge to enlist as a hospital orderly, while his colleagues (some of them) toiled at desks in British Intelligence during the Second World War. In his twenties he was true to his Austrian roots, and later he was true to his recently grafted British roots. He had a primitive, non-intellectualized hold on something he should be true to, something that was real to which he should witness. He lacked any articulate or systematic basis for regarding that witness as a witness to truth rather than to illusion or falsehood. Yet his actions showed that in his fifties he could be true to British soil without being false to Austrian terrain, and he could be true to Austrian terrain (earlier) without desecrating British soil. His later British loyalties were not a self-betrayal.

How is it so easy to malign truth, call it an illusion, deny that there is such a thing? Can't we say Wittgenstein was true to his roots? Well, perhaps he joined up for a less exalted reason: say he wished to undermine a fear that he was an arrogant privileged aristocrat above the call of common duty? But if that is true, we wouldn't be maligning truth, we'd just be arguing that *someone* could be true to his roots, but that was not true of *Wittgenstein*. We'd still have a robust notion of truth in play.

Wittgenstein read Kierkegaard and called him the greatest philosopher of the nineteenth century—better than Marx, Schopenhauer, or Nietzsche. We could say that Kierkegaard remained true to Christian roots even as he was true to his pagan, Socratic roots. To say that would be to keep a robust notion of truth in play. Kierkegaard was an unrepentant admirer of Socrates. A pagan could tell him something about how he should live, about where his loyalties lay. He knew he was fully Christian and fully Socratic, and that neither loyalty betrayed the other. Neither Christ nor Socrates, as he saw it, put much stock in winning anyone to a creed. He could be true to the paths they followed, though one path was Christian and the other non-Christian. He remained true to a path that crisscrossed wildly between Athens and Jerusalem. We might find integrity in his living while we puzzled how one could make sense of an amalgam of Christ and Socrates.

Truth gets maligned. We hear on the streets and in the academy that it's an empty idol, that with the death of God we must also accept the death of truth. But does that mean it's useless to wonder if there's a true path one should follow, that we should think it's bogus to say Kierkegaard was true to a Christian path and true to a Pagan path, or that Wittgenstein was true to his Austrian roots, and then true to his British roots? Of course, we might discover that Kierkegaard betrayed his Christian or Pagan roots, but then we'd still be maintaining a robust philosophical sense of truth. The notion of being true to something in one's life isn't jejune.

EPILOGUE: TRUTHS IN THE TRENCHES

When someone speaks truthfully or acts on what she takes to be true to her path, or true to who she is, we have a notion of truth in play that allows us to speak of the integrity or virtue of Socrates, Kierkegaard, or Wittgenstein. Each, we could say, bears witness to something, in action and comportment. Each bears witness to a good. This is a noble sort of truthfulness, a truth embedded in character and ways of life. How do we come to recognize a good life—recognize that Socrates acts truly, that not caving before the Athenian public and not escaping his death sentence as his friends urge him to do, is not self-betrayal, but self-consolidation, integrity, being true to himself? This is a truth to cherish. Truth is not a hollow shell we toss aside as we become philosophically sophisticated, skeptical, and perhaps cynical.

On his deathbed, at the conclusion of what can only be called a tormented life, Wittgenstein asked his comforter, "Please tell them I've had a wonderful life." He spoke truthfully, I'm sure, though that witness was nothing that he, or anyone else, could confirm as true. He spoke truly, witnessed truly. I often imagine Kierkegaard witnessing from his deathbed, despite his Christian torments, "Tell them I've had a wonderful, wonderfully Socratic life." The moral here is that a plurality of truths is not evidence for the absence of truths—or truth. This is an error Nietzsche and others can fall into. To say that truth is perspectival, always delivered from a perspective, does not entail that there is no truth. From the perspective of an ant, humans are very large—that's a truth; and from the perspective of a whale, humans are not that large at all—that's a truth.

Speaking at Syracuse, Hélène Cixous confided the sweet touch of shared words over the years with Jacques Derrida. She was a true friend to him as he lived and a true friend to bring him alive, as she did, far from Paris that day. She delivered truth to those with ears to hear: a resonant truth, a tactile truth, a truth that touched and blossomed from touch. Like Kierkegaard and Wittgenstein, she witnessed truly to a quality of life. Truth matters.

Speaking in a large public stadium in the wake of 9/11, a Lutheran pastor shared a space of prayer with Imams and Rabbis and Priests, witnessing not to friendship but to true and truthful communion across sectarian lines. In distain of such truth, he was defrocked forthwith. Witness is not trouble-free. Through his comportment, he embraced Islam and Judaism while wedded to Christianity. He might have whispered, "Tell them that there, for the moment, I was Muslim and Jew." He was truly exemplary of solidarity in mourning and compassion, across faiths and non-faiths.

Truth matters. We yearn for it and we're up to our necks in untruth. Disparaging Big Truth, Richard Rorty left a constraining Princeton for a looser Virginia, and then moved on to hang-loose California. Harry Frankfurt speaks for tactile truths from Princeton in a little book called *Bull Shit*. If you want to expose BS, you'd better believe in truth. Truth is triumphant as BS gets outed. It glows also in true witness, true communion, true friendship, true service—in being true to oneself and others. My apprentice must "true up" the juncture of that beam and its support. Perhaps it's asking too much to have politicians live truly, but we want John Wayne to have true grit. To dump truth is to dump the goodness of Wittgenstein's service, the beauty of Cixoux's friendship, the witness of a Lutheran pastor, the incisiveness of Frankfurt's polemic against BS. To scorn truth is to leave untruth standing. If a madman cries out that truth is dead, you can block your ears or send him away.

Against theory

We don't need a theory of truth to grasp truths of witness, communion, or friendship any more than we need a theory of music to grasp Beethoven's invincibility, his immortality. We don't need a theory to grasp Thoreau's witness to the Concord and Merrimack as revelatory sites of truths. Knowing the landscape, we have an instinctive grasp of BS (Frankfurt helps us sharpen it).

Knowing the field, we have a grasp of the quarterback's true vision, true grace under fire. Doing considerable reading in Thoreau country, we can grasp the truths of his witness—in writing, walking, and civil resistance.

Getting to religion's tactile truths is getting around in the landscapes of prayers, tears, and apocalypse; getting the feel of confession, pieties, and beloved mothers; of absent fathers, envies, loyalties, fear, and trembling. These terrains are enlivened as we trace how Buddha or Jesus or Gandhi cut through them, interrupting and disrupting and reassembling as they go. We get a knack for their witness to the lay of the land and to the things and practices it embraces. We move among tactile truths.

The thought of tactile truth is linked to Wallace Stevens's invitation to let poetry give us "Not ideas about the thing, but the thing itself." And to be given "the thing itself" is a gift to touch, not an idea about what touches us. For Thoreau, death appears on a Fire Island beach as the bones of his friend Margaret Fuller, close enough to touch. He works for a harmony of head and heart, ear and eye, nose—and hand.

A few years ago, at a conference at Wheaton College, a speaker evoked El Capitan's walls in Yosemite as a site where a climber could have tactile knowledge of an exhilarating, timeless moment, an *Augenblick*, or series of them, high above the valley floor. There was witness to tactile truths revealed to the living body, truths of the most extraordinary kind, available nowhere else and in no other way than by inching one's way up the granite face 'til a thousand feet dropped off below, and thousands more beckoned above. Truth spoke from the rocks and the climber alike—from the skies—and to those viewing rooted in the meadows below. The moral is that tactile truths, and witness to them, get us through the night.

Pilate asks, *What Is Truth*? but his interlocutor ducks, as he should. The question is doubly mocking, of truths and of the exemplar before him. If my son gathers his equipment to attempt an ascent that I think he's ill-prepared for, I won't halt him at the curb and ask "What is truth?" I'd ask, if he were young and ill-prepared, "What's up with your foolhardy ways? Why shouldn't I ground you?" Pilate is also asking, but of Jesus, "What's up with your foolhardy ways? Why shouldn't I ground you, or worse?" He needs a tactile sense, a grip on what's up with an ill-dressed man who, it's rumored, witnesses to being all that a true human being is and should be, who comports himself as an exemplar for others. Perhaps his detractors fancy that he takes himself to be a true king relative to others. Pilate wants a story to tell, to himself and any who might question him later, about what's up with this trouble-maker/prophet/teller-of-parables/harmless-miracle-worker/delusional-self-styled-king/insufficiently-humble-wanderer/disrupter-of-the-temple-stock-exchange—what's up with this person who says he's the way and the truth—what's up with him, and what will he, Pilate, do about it.

On my view, Pilate couldn't care less about the truth that good academics in theology and philosophy ask graduate students about in PhD qualifying exams. In their allotted hours, our good students run the gauntlet: "What is truth?" Well, let's look at skeptics, conventionalists, pragmatists, deconstructionists, pre-postmodernists, semanticists, Platonists, nominalists, Aristotelians, etc., etc. What's wrong with this picture? Well, this is precisely *not* truth-seeking—but *why*? Truth-seeking culminates in a witness to truth or to its absence. It does not culminate in a *theory* about truth.

For a theory of truth, we assume that there's a neutral "view from nowhere" from which we can announce "there is no truth" or "truth is what works" or "truth is the interest of the stronger" or "truth is a distillate of gender, history, and genes—not to mention a distillate of party affiliation, income, and having or not having resolved one's Oedipal issues." Or "truth is a distillate of anyone's mood, his mood of the moment." But I'll get off this train, if you please. There's something deeply untrue in the direction these tracks are going. I'm not skeptical about truth. I'm skeptical of proceeding at this nonliving level of generality, at this great distance from the street, from the trenches.

"Is it true that Derrida had an aversion to binaries?"—I can handle that. I'll consult texts and come up with something at least passable. "Is it true that binaries bully our perceptions and discourses?" I'm not clueless about how to argue, one way or the other. "Does JD smuggle in a false absolute, the 'absolute truth' that you can't get deeper than binaries—or is his view here just an offhand remark that he'd retract in a moment?" I can handle all this. Truth has a grip, there's a road and the rubber—one hits the other. However, if I hear yet again, "But come, just what is this … this *truth of the matter* that you so confidently invoke?"—if I hear that, I shut down. I head for the door. Or get shrill or insistent. The question sounds deep but is in fact bloviation.

Asking about truth is not asking about One-Big-Thing, but asking about true witness, true friendship, true communion—no more, no less. It's asking about true liars and true BSers, in the White House or anywhere—about true heroes and true villains; it's asking whether binaries push us around or whether global warming is upon us—no more, no less. There is no Big Question about Truth left over, still to tackle, after thinking about these truths (or falsities) from the street. There is no Big Question about Truth—say how to define that Big Thing—that we have to answer before we dig in to ponder true witness, true friendship, and so forth. If someone persists "But what is truth—in general, overall?" then we should, like the good Socrates, artfully change the subject, or tactfully get off the train. Or offer very modest, push-cart versions: "a 'true X' is the best of its kind"—whether a true musician or true Christian, a true description or a true scholar. To give the idea a range of application, from low to high, I'd offer a parallel push-cart version: "a true X is a legitimate instance of its kind"—not a counterfeit or a forgery, but not necessarily the best of its kind.

I'd stick with push-cart versions, but not because Big Truth is a messy and difficult part of the city. I'd get off the train advertising Big Truth as destination because like Gertrude Stein will say of Oakland—"There's no *there* there"—no there to go to. To knit one's brow and worry the question "What is truth?" is to try to think from a supra-celestial nowhere, surveying all time and eternity. It's to try to think oneself into divinity. More ornately, to ask The Big Question is to beg a release from Dasein, a release from Heidegger's "there-ness." It's to presume exemption from the only field from which sensible questions about truth can be safely launched.

"What is truth?"—overall, in general—is a rootless, hopeless, slightly inane question. It flutters weightlessly in gossip and chatter. Emerson anticipates wonderfully. "We are place," he announces. That is, we are not gods, not disembodied consciousness, not exempt from placement, from the street, the trenches, or the village. Thoreau would agree—from a pond not far from the village of Concord.

Tactile truth

Getting truths from the trenches (or the streets) calls for a kind of tactile ability to sense what to trust and what to mistrust, what's exemplary and what's third-rate, what's "true love," "true friendship," "true pitch," "true aim"—and what's a shoddy simulacrum. Working toward the genuine, toward the shining exemplar, is a knack, something we pick up—or don't. Some can't miss a shill or a conman. Others predictably do. Some light up at a true cabernet, others don't. Some see Jesus as king, others won't. Some will hear genius in Dickinson and others will miss it. There's a knack for tactile truths, visceral truths. We get it from the streets, or in classrooms or under temple roofs or Concord skies. We are the place where these truths get worked out and negotiated, where we absorb their touch and scent and ring. The truths we have a knack for detecting are not true propositions we can pocket and consult when we're lost. Having a knack for the tactile ones allows us to hear the truth in Wittgenstein's deathbed words, "Tell them I've had a wonderful life," or to grasp the truth in his honoring newly grafted British roots, or to grasp the truth that he doesn't thereby uproot his Austrian ones. With this knack, we hear Cixoux's celebration of friendship.

Is truth objectivity? In science, in law courts, in serious journalism, we aim to attain it. We aim for objectivity, and when we achieve or approach it, we pride ourselves on realizing some passable degree of it. In science, law courts, or serious journalism we aim for objectivity in reports and descriptions, because in those contexts, objectivity is the genuine thing to pursue, the real thing, the best of its kind. If we miss objectivity, we feel shame.

Is truth subjectivity? It is when conscience insists that I be true to what I am and must be as a human being, insists that I probe and weigh my passionate investments, and not refuse an awareness that I count for something and that the world can surprise. Subjectivity is, among other things, acknowledging responsibility, and that's a good thing, something to be true to. To answer for oneself is an individual imperative that flows primitively from me, not from the "objective" spirit of culture or city or commonplace gestures and platitudes of the time.

Truth is objectivity; truth is subjectivity. A deep personal investment in honest scientific research weds subjective truth and objective truth. Einstein's embrace of Relativity coupled his embrace of objective truth with witness to subjective truth, so tightly was his identity coiled around it. And some truths are perhaps neither one nor the other. I have a true taste for Camembert and Richter has a true touch for Schubert, but these truths are neither the outcome of reliable, verifiable reporting nor a responsible witness to a personal investment. And there's the subtle point that an ear for BS is something other than an ear for the absence of objective truth. It's closer to having an ear for the *betrayal* of the subjective truth that truth *matters* to me. We learn to sort the sham from the real, the true from the false, the deep from the shallow. We learn to sort the objective from the subjective and the instances of neither and both. To sort is to have a knack for attunement to the varied landscapes I pass through. Learning music is getting the gist of its spirit, the gist of true pitch, true expression, true regard for a composer and for one's fellow performers.

Religious truth, or truths in religion

It's best to think of religions on the street rather than seek them and their truths sequestered in heavenly raptures. Does the rubber hit the road when we look for religious truths? It's best to steer away from the hopeless question "Which religion is true?"—and away from the presumption that Pilate's question makes sense, and away from the illusion that if we only knew the answer, we could adjudicate other people's lives in light of that answer. There is no such light or answer. What we can do is to steer for an insider's knack. We need a knack for the truth, not of a bulk item, "religion," but for the tactile truth of the singular lilt of a Haiku, of the feel of a prayer shawl, of the taste of communion bread and wine, of the ornate patterns of tile work in a cathedral in Byzantium.

Little is gained philosophically by a fixation on the spectacular clashes of one so-called religion with another. And to minimize the debilitating fallout from such clashes, we need to stay in the trenches, work harder for the tactile feel of ways of singing, praying, burying, wedding, blessing, forgiving, praising, meditating, walking, dressing, eating—and how these weave in and out of things holy and sacred, polluted and corrupt. Staying in trenches means learning aspects of Quaker quiet and of Orthodox iconography and of Staretz Silouan on Hell and Despair. It's to have a feel for Buddha on the afflictions of age and wealth. It's being able to smile with a hermit as he confides, with a twinkle, "My Lord told me a joke. And seeing him laugh has done more for me than any scripture I will ever read."

If I'm worried about religious sensibilities or truths that seem strange or threatening to me, it wouldn't help to ask, "What is truth?" It wouldn't help to head off on a NEH-funded research program. I'd ask, at street level, from the trenches, "May I listen in?" "May I sit with you?" That might lessen the chasms between my sensibilities and yours, letting me get some small knack of your sense of true friends, true prayer, true blessing, true dance. That won't close all the gaps between us; nothing can, and probably nothing should.

At the level of institutional conflict, it's doubtful that having a more intimate sense of another's religious truths will eliminate violence, though it might bring the level down a notch, for a moment. But we should no more expect theories of truth or immersion in another's ways of life to bring contesting religions together, than we should expect theories of truth or immersion in other's ways to bring warfare or hatred or greed to a quick end.

Let me close with two instances where I've had small but important glimmers of hope—places where rubber hits the road, and one knows one has hit something significant.

A recent graduate of Duke, Peter Dula now has a book, on Cavell and theology. A pacifist, he served a year in neighborhood shelters in Iraq with the war going full tilt. We'd learn more from his tactile sense of truths—truths of hope and faith under fire—than we would, I suspect, from reading a thousand essays on truth and pluralism. The truths he can witness to resonate with the cry of Starets Silouan: "Keep your mind in Hell, and Despair not!" His witness is Gandhi's or Simone Weil's.

Now I think of a woman wearing a Muslim scarf. She sits quietly in a summer class I lead at a local Catholic College. She'll teach me something without uttering a word. I have no theory of truth or handbook for negotiating religious difference. I'll be alert to an assigned Melville text in new ways. I'll linger with the delight Ishmael and Queequeg take in each other in their room at the Spouter-Inn. One celebrates Ramadan, the other Christmas, one shyly covers his feet, the other shyly covers up other parts. One sleeps with a knife, the other doesn't. One drapes his arm comfortably over his bedmate; the other is terrified. They become best of friends.

Queequeg invites Ishmael to join in his pagan ritual. Without batting an eye, Ishmael thinks: "I would do as I would have done to me—I would have Queequeg join me in prayer; I will join him in prayer." He arrives at a tactile truth, not unlike that of our good Lutheran pastor, and all for the good. My scarfed student listens.

No doubt I'd have a sixth sense working as I get students thinking of this scene—a sixth sense, to monitor my scarfed student's response, revealed, perhaps overtly, perhaps in a subtlety—in her face or eyes, in a stiffening or relaxing of her posture. At another point I might bring up Muslims opening their Mosque as shelter for persecuted Christians in thirteenth-century Spain—one Christian rabble fleeing another. The persecuted were saved, for a moment, hidden. There was nowhere to go. Muslims opened their doors.

To knit one's brow and worry the question "What is truth?" is to try to think from a supra-celestial nowhere, surveying all time and eternity. It's to try to think oneself into divinity. More ornately, to ask The Big Question is to beg a release from *Dasein*, a release from Heidegger's "there-ness." It's to presume exemption from the only field from which sensible questions about truth can be safely launched.

"What is truth?" Overall, in general? This is a rootless, slightly inane question. It flutters weightlessly in gossip and chatter. Emerson anticipates wonderfully. "We are place," he announces. That is, we are not gods, not disembodied consciousness, not exempt from placement, not detached from the street or the village or the trenches. Thoreau would agree—from a pond not far from the village of Concord.

If we are place, what is our place? Our place is the place that addresses us, and the place that addresses us (me) enjoins a regard for truth. It will have no truck with lies and falsehoods. The oak or the neighbor or the sunset have no use for dissimulation; they require my frank response. If I am the context, the place of my friend's address, that friend can insist that I be true. We hope persons with religious sensibilities admire true human beings outside the circle of their practice, and if we are outsiders to each other, we might still ponder the true aims of prayer, confession, or prophecy. It is our place to be moved by gestures of true friendship or true solidarity, to acknowledge the true magnificence of granite walls, or of a truly ripe Camembert. It's truly our place to respect the quiet of another's prayer and listen to chants in languages we don't understand.

The moral is that I know many of these truths of appreciation and comportment like the back of my hand. Might I be wrong? Of course! Might I be right, some, or most of the time? I'd better believe it.

NOTES

Chapter 1

1 Kelly Dean Jolley, *Stony Lonesome* (Auburn, AL: New Plains Press, 2014).

2 *Appalachian Mountain Club White Mountain Guide*, ed. (Boston, MA: AMC Books, 1976), 3.

3 Stanley Cavell, *Philosophy the Day after Tomorrow* (Cambridge, MA: Harvard University Press, 2005), 186–87.

4 Dante begins *The Divine Comedy* finding himself midway in his life in a dark wood.

5 W. E. Hocking, unpublished Gifford Lectures, 1941.

6 David Rothenberg, *Sudden Music: Improvisation, Sound, Nature* (Athens: University Georgia Press, 2002), 123.

7 E. F. Mooney, "Preservative Care: Saving Intimate Voice in the Humanities," in *Lost Intimacy in American Thought: Recovering Personal Philosophy from Thoreau to Cavell* (London: Continuum, 2009).

8 "A performative utterance is an offer of participation in the order of law. And perhaps we can say: A passionate utterance is an invitation to improvisation in the disorders of desire." Stanley Cavell, "Passionate and Performative Utterance," in *Contending with Stanley Cavell*, ed. Russell B. Goodman (Oxford: Oxford University Press, 2005), Ch. 10, 192–3.

9 Stanley Cavell, *Little Did I Know: Excerpts from Memory* (Stanford, CA: Stanford University Press, 2010). William Day, "A Soteriology of Reading: Cavell's *Excerpts from Memory*," in *Stanley Cavell, Literature, and Criticism*, ed. Andrew Taylor (Manchester: Manchester University Press, 2011).

10 "The Availability" is reprinted in *Stanley Cavell. Must We Mean What We Say: A Book of Essays* (Cambridge: Cambridge University Press, 1976), Ch. 2. This early essay is an invitation to read *Philosophical Investigations* in an existential and theological light.

11 I listen to *what* is said, *how* it is said, and how it *elicits* my own sensibilities and soul. *What* is said could be a simple declaration "*Be yourself.*" We get the dictionary meaning of each word if not a message. *How* it is said begins to fill in meaning

beyond mere recitation of sounds. It might be *rebuking* ("Stop playing the clown!" Or, *encouraging*. "Just relax, you'll do fine!"). Third, I might register my *existential* response. As I hear, "*Be Yourself!*" I might ask if I *personally avoid*—or *embrace* or am just *baffled* by "*Be Yourself!*"

12 George Eliot, *Middlemarch* (many editions), Ch. 20. She senses danger in contact with the otherness of things.

13 Biblical ethics can raise the most profound questions while refusing satisfying answers.

14 We learn promises (a paradigmatic "performative" as Austin introduces the term) first as making and marking a "promising bond"—to parents and siblings, for instance. As a child grows, one part of "the self" can make promises to another: one can vow or promise oneself to be a better violinist or listener. Epigrammatically: "the 'having' of a self is being the other to one's self, calling upon it with the words of others." Stanley Cavell, *Philosophical Passages, Wittgenstein, Emerson, Austin, Derrida* (New Jersey: Wiley-Blackwell, 1995), 102.

15 Henry James, "The Middle Years," in *The Tales of Henry James*, ed. Edward Wagenknecht (New York: Frederick Ungar, 1984).

Chapter 2

1 Martin Heidegger, *Hegel's Phenomenology of Spirit*, trans. Kevin Maly et al. (Bloomington: Indiana University Press, 1988), 42.

2 John Hermann Randall, "F. H. Bradley and the Working-Out of Absolute Idealism," *Journal for History of Philosophy* 5, no. 3 (July 1967) describing Bradley's *Appearance and Reality*.

3 Kierkegaard wants to bypass objectivist philosophy by restoring a sense of the presence of words, selves, and the world. This is part of the broad project of romantic re-enchantment. For a wonderful discussion, see Antony Rudd, "Wittgenstein and Heidegger as Romantic Modernists," in *Wittgenstein and Heidegger*, ed. Egan et. al. (Abingdon: Routledge, 2013).

4 The epigraph was written with F. H. Bradley in mind. Of course, much of Kierkegaard is dialectics or religious poeticizing, but these genres can overlap theater.

5 Wittgenstein writes, "[The] Spirit of a book has to be evident in the Book itself, and can't be described. It is a Great Temptation to try to make the Spirit Explicit," in

Culture and Value (New York: Blackwell, 1984), 6. By the book's "spirit" he means the book's presence.

6. "Kierkegaard created [his novel] position by merging Hegel's insistence that we must have some kind of contact with anything we can call real (thus rejecting the noumenal), with Kant's belief that reality fundamentally exceeds our understanding; human reason should not be the criterion of the real. The result is the idea that our most vivid encounters with reality come in experiences that shatter our categories." Braver Lee, "A Brief History of Continental Realism," *Continental Philosophy Review* 45 (2012): 261–289, 15.

7. In a museum, a landscape painting catches my eye. To take in *more* of it, I won't rush to determine the painter' dates or a critic's view of technique.

8. Søren Kierkegaard, *Concluding Unscientific Postscript*, trans. Howard and Edna Hong (Princeton: Princeton University Press, 1992). Original Danish edition, 1846. (Søren Kierkegaard's Skrifter Volume 7): Kierkegaard, Søren, and Niels Jørgen. Cappelørn. Afsluttende Uvidenskabelig Efterskrift. Kierkegaard, Søren, 1813–1855. Works. 1997; 7. København: Gad, 2002. Neither the *Wikipedia* article on Kierkegaard nor the Amazon listings give the full title.

9. This rendering is suggested by Alastair Hannay, *Kierkegaard, A Biography* (Cambridge: Cambridge University Press, 2002), 315.

10. This is true despite *Postscript* technical distinctions, for instance between religiousness A and B, or between history and faith.

11. Hannay, *Kierkegaard, A Biography*.

12. *The Odyssey*, trans. Robert Fagles (New York: Penguin, 1997).

13. In the final pages of *Postscript*, Climacus *revokes* all he has written. Taking something back can be slapstick and cruel. I give you a sparkling invitation. Then, to your chagrin (and my audience's callous delight), I grab it back, revoke it. April fool! Hegel thought dialectic was always progressive and forward moving. Revocation is backward moving. See my "*Postscript*: Humor takes it Back," in *On Søren Kierkegaard* (Aldershot: Ashgate, 2007).

14. Braver, "A Brief History of Continental Realism."

15. Mystery here is not simple ignorance nor a ploy to shut down questioning. It's holding our breath in wonder or awe or fear, and not disposed of or overcome by better knowledge.

16. Salmon Rushdie, *The Ground Beneath Her Feet* (London: Picador, 2000), 19. See my "Saving Intimate Voice," in *Lost Intimacy in American Thought* (New York: Continuum, 2009), 163.

17. Heidegger, *Hegel's Phenomenology of Spirit*.

18 Ibid. Kelly Dean Jolley: "It is fascinating how this passage resonates with the Preface passage in *Philosophical Investigations* where Wittgenstein talks of his picture of the essence of the book he wants to write, and then recounts how he came to repent of the picture when he realized that the inner form of his book was the inner necessity of the book's issue itself." (Personal note.)

19 Ludwig Wittgenstein, *Philosophical Investigations* (London: Blackwell, 1973), section 122.

20 See "*Postscript*: Humor takes it back."

21 Attributed to Rabbi Simcha Bunim of Peschischa: "Everyone must have two pockets, with a note in each pocket, so that he or she can reach into the one or the other, depending on the need. When feeling lowly and depressed, discouraged or disconsolate, one should reach into the right pocket, and, there, find the words: "For my sake was the world created." But when feeling high and mighty one should reach into the left pocket and find the words: 'I am but dust and ashes.'" Martin Buber, *Tales of the Hasidim: Later Masters* (New York: Schocken Books, 1948), 249.

22 See my "Style and Pseudonymity," in *Excursions with Kierkegaard* (New York: Bloomsbury, 2013), Ch. 3.

23 See what I call, after Bakhtin, "The Carnivalesque Sublime," in *Excursions*. 61.

24 Braver, "A Brief History of Continental Realism."

Chapter 4

1 E. F. Mooney, ed., *Wilderness and the Heart* (Athens: University of Georgia Press, 1999), vii.

2 Borgmann, personal note. *The Inward Morning* (New York: Harper and Row 1976); first published by Bald Eagle Press, 1958.

3 See Borgmann, *Inward Morning*, back cover blurbs.

4 Cf. David Rodick, *Wilderness in America* (New York: Fordham University Press, 2017), 187.

5 Rodick, *Wilderness in America*, 18.

6 There are many translations of Job 40 (his "quieting"): KJV: *Then Job answered and said: "Behold, I am vile; What shall I answer You? I lay my hand over my mouth."* I prefer Fingarette's, "*I melt away.*" See *Revisions*, Hauerwas & MacIntyre, eds. (Notre Dame: University of Notre Dame Press, 1983), 249–86.

7   Herder, trans., *Dimensions of Job*, ed. Nahum Glatzner (New York: Schocken, 1969), 149.

8   Borgmann, *Inward Morning*, 139.

9   Ibid., 140.

10 Ibid.

11 These words appeared in memorial notes at a gathering after Bugbee's death.

12 Kelly Dean Jolley (*Quantum Est In Rebus Inane*, Blog, June 2013)

Chapter 5

1   Herman Melville, *Moby-Dick; or, The Whale*, eds. Harrison Hyaford, Hershel Parker, and G. Thomas Tanselle (Evanston: Northwestern University Press, 1988), 374.

2   Ibid., 5.

3   Ibid., 276.

4   Ibid., 183.

5   Ibid., 164.

6   Ibid., 195.

7   Ibid., 107.

8   D. M. MacKinnon, "Death," in *New Essays in Philosophical Theology*, ed. Flew and MacIntyre (New York: St. Martins, 1966), 266.

9   See the Epilogue, below.

10 Ibid., 573.

11 Edward F. Mooney, *Lost Intimacy in American Thought: Recovering Personal Philosophy from Thoreau to Cavell* (London: Ashgate, 2009).

12 There are truths in objectivity, and truths in subjectivity. See my *On Søren Kierkegaard: Dialogue, Polemic, Lost Intimacy and Time* (London: Ashgate, 2007).

13 In *The Senses of Walden* (Chicago: University Chicago Press, 1992), 33, Cavell asks if the pinnacle of American philosophy arrives in "the metaphysical riot" of nineteenth-century literature.

14 Melville, *Moby-Dick; or, The Whale*, 320.

15 Ibid.

16 Ibid., 497.

17 I'd call this "Natural-Supernaturalism" or "Natural-Transcendentalism." However, "Supernaturalism" and "Transcendentalism" resonate with otherworldliness. See my *Excursions with Thoreau: Philosophy, Poetry, Religion* (London: Bloomsbury, 2015). For romanticism and the re-enchantment of nature, see Anthony Rudd, "Wittgenstein and Heidegger as Romantic Modernists," in *Wittgenstein and Heidegger*, ed. Egan et al. (Abingdon: Routledge, 2013).

18 Melville, *Moby-Dick; or, The Whale*, 449.

19 Ibid., 491.

20 Ibid., 492.

21 Ibid., 374.

22 Ibid., 492. See my *Excursions with Thoreau*.

23 Ramadan should be a *day*-long fast—Melville takes liberties.

24 Ibid., 62.

25 Ibid., 81.

26 Ibid., 85.

27 Ibid., 123.

28 Revision of "Passion, Reverie, Disaster, Joy: What Philosophers Learn at Sea," in *Melville among the Philosophers*, ed. Corey McCall (Lexington: Lexington Press, 2018).

Chapter 6

1 *Moby-Dick*, 508.

2 Ibid.

3 Ibid.

4 Ibid., 507.

5 Ibid.

6 Ibid., 571–72.

7 Ibid., 508.

8 Ibid., 389.

9 Ibid., 433.

10 *Hamlet* (Act 2, Scene 2); Polonius spoofs scholars forcing literary works into categories. Shakespeare William, *The Arden Shakespeare edition* (New York: Bloomsbury, 2016).

11 See my discussion of Job above, Ch. 4.

12 *Moby-Dick*, 388.

13 Rowan Williams: "Loss is 'imprecise'. Nothing serious, grievous, in our humanity allows us the satisfaction of being exact, wrapping it all up. What we do with bereavement is to find words that 'turn things about.'" See *PN Review*, Vol. 43, No. 2, November-December 2016, 232.

14 Robert Alter translates *tohu wabohu* as "waste and welter." See *Genesis: a New Translation* (New York: Norton, 1997).

15 Genesis 50:26. Bible, *New Standard Revised, 1989.*

16 *Moby-Dick*, 343.

17 This is a farcical allusion to Jonah reborn from the *mouth* of a whale.

18 *Moby-Dick,* 319.

19 Ibid., 573.

20 Ibid., 522.

21 Ibid.

22 *Moby-Dick*, 492. This immediately follows: "There is no steady unretracing progress in this life; we do not advance through fixed gradations, and at the last one pause:—through infancy's unconscious spell, boyhood's thoughtless faith, adolescence" doubt (the common doom), then scepticism, then disbelief, resting at last in manhood's pondering repose of If. But once gone through, we trace the round again; and are infants, boys, and men, and Ifs eternally."

23 Ibid., 492.

24 Ibid., 167.

25 Ibid., 571. Ishmael has moments of moderate uncertainty: "all have doubts; many deny; but doubts or denials, few along with them, have intuitions. Doubts of all things earthly, and intuitions of some things heavenly; this combination makes neither believer nor infidel, but makes a man who regards them both with equal eye." (374)

26 Ibid., 492.

27 Ibid., 492.

28 Ibid., 567.

29 Ibid., 388. Women are absent, yet nursing, mothering, and childbirth enter in a heart-stopping scene that brings killing to a halt: the crew responds in awe to

the ocean nursery, mothers and newborns swimming in circles. Childbirth and midwifery appear in Queequeg's delivery of Tashtego from a whale's womb-like spouting channel (343). Queequeg and Ishmael sleep in a loving embrace usually reserved for wife and husband (25).

30 Ibid., 387.
31 Ibid., 389.
32 Ibid., 388.
33 Ibid., 389. Cf. "Joy is the condition of life." Henry David Thoreau, "The Natural History of Massachusetts," in *Collected Essays and Poems of Thoreau*, ed. Elizabeth Hall Witherell (New York: Library of America, 2001), 22.
34 Ibid., 416.
35 Revised portion of "Passion, Reverie, Disaster, Joy: What Philosophers Learn at Sea," *Melville among the Philosophers*, ed. Corey McCall (Lexington: Lexington Books, 2018).

Chapter 7

1 See David Brooks on Jane Addams: *New York Times*, April 25, 2017.
2 See Edward F. Mooney "Style and Pseudonyms in Kierkegaard's Authorship," in *Oxford Handbook to Kierkegaard*, ed. John Lippitt and George Pattison (Oxford: Oxford University Press, 2013).
3 Nor are we encouraged to believe that Abraham should have doubted it was really God who spoke. And for Johannes de silentio, the prevalence of child sacrifice in Abraham's era doesn't count, one way or the other, in coming to understand Abraham's faith.
4 Philosophers have argued that values can be objective rather than subjective. Whether one endorses or affirms them is nevertheless an "existential" or "subjective" issue. Kierkegaard is focused on personal endorsing and affirming, not whether values are objective or subjective.
5 Kierkegaard is read as supporting "inwardness," but a better rendering would be "heartfelt-ness" or, in Hannay's suggestion, "cordiality."
6 This is "inter-subjectivity," but that's not a Kierkegaardian term of art.
7 *Fear and Trembling*, trans. Hannay, 95, 145f. Cf. Wittgenstein, "Faith Is a Passion, While Wisdom Is Cool Grey Ash," in *Culture and Value* (Chicago: University of Chicago, 1984), 56C.

8   The *Postscript* is written by the pseudonym Johannes Climacus, someone apparently climbing up into Christianity, perhaps with a Socratic, questioning sensibility, and deeply moral.

9   In Danish, "Kierkegaard" is "church grave yard"—"kierke," church, plus "gaard," yard.

10 *Postscript*, trans. Hannay, 197.

11 The coming-of-night and an-uncanny-mist are throbing subjectivities.

12 Pattison: nature "signals a kind of transcendence" that evokes "the anxiety of self-relation." See his "Kierkegaard and the Sublime," *Kierkegaard Studies Yearbook* 3 (1998): 245–75.

13 *Postscript*, 171.

14 Ibid., 197.

15 Wittgenstein: "[The] spirit of a book has to be evident in the book itself, and can't be described … It is a great temptation to try to make the spirit explicit" (*Culture and Value*, 6, 7). By the book's "spirit" he means the book's *presence*. Talking about the crash or cackle of words evokes their presence—the opposite of making the spirit of word explicit.

16 Heidegger, *Hegel's Phenomenology*, 42.

17 Randall, "F. H. Bradley and the Working-Out of Absolute Idealism"; describing Bradley's *Appearance and Reality*. See Kelly Dean Jolley's blog, *Quantum est in Rebus Inane*, March 22, 2016.

18 Kierkegaard wants to bypass objectivist philosophy by restoring the presence of words, selves, and the world. This is part of the broader project of romantic re-enchantment of the world. See Rudd, "Wittgenstein and Heidegger as Romantic Modernists."

Chapter 8

1   *Kierkegaard's Papers and Journals, a Selection*, ed. Alastair Hannay (New York: Penguin, 1996), 33.

2   Jaokim Garff, *Søren Kierkegaard: A Biography*, trans. Bruce Kirmmse (Princeton: Princeton University Press, 2005).

3   Sartre's theory of radical choice may have its roots here. See Mooney, 2001.

4   See Ch. 9, "Seductions and My Circus Identity."

5   *Fear and Trembling*, 44

6   Exodus 4:24–26

7   *Fear and Trembling*, 66.

8   A merely objective existence would have no *there* there—as Gertrude Stein said of Oakland.

9   Søren Kierkegaard, Sickness Unto Death, ed and trans. Alastair Hannay, New York, Penguin Books, 1989, 43.

10 Mooney, 2013.

11 Pattison, personal note.

12 *Fear and Trembling*, 68f.

13 This image is sung in Kierkegaard's "The Lilies of the Field and the Birds of the Air."

14 This is a revised version of "Kierkegaard" in *Religion and European Philosophy: Key Thinkers from Kant to the Present*, ed. Phillip Goodchild and Hollis Phelps (Abingdon: Routledge, 2015).

Chapter 9

1   William Stringfellow, *Essential Writings* (Maryknoll, N.Y.: Orbis, 2013), 209.

Chapter 10

1   *Fear and Trembling*, 68–70.

2   I limit my discussion to the improvisational sketches in *Fear and Trembling*. The theme of faithful living crisscrosses the Kierkegaardian corpus, first to last. However, looking for a generic account of faith is as flawed as looking for a generic "Bach Theme." There's no substitute for listening attentively to particular Bach passages—whether culled from arias, suites, or full Passions. Just so, there is no substitute for listening attentively to particular Kierkegaard phrases, passages, and lyrical improvisations of the sort we find so artfully rendered in *Fear and Trembling*.

3   *Fear and Trembling*, 68–69.

4   *Philosophy and Animal Life*, Diamond Cavell et al. (New York: Columbia University Press, 2009), Ch. 1.

5   *Fear and Trembling*, 94.

6   Ibid., 70.

7   The man "looks just like a tax-collector." *Fear and Trembling*, 68.

8   Agnes (in the third *Problema*) also wrestles with faith.

9   John Davenport takes up Tolkien's discussion of eucatastrophy in "Faith as Eschatological Trust in *Fear and Trembling*," in *Ethics, Love, and Faith in Kierkegaard: A Philosophical Engagement*, ed. Edward F. Mooney (Bloomington: Indiana University Press 2008), 196–233.

10 Hannay renders the Danish title ("*Stemning*") of this opening section "attunement."

11 The cover of the Penguin edition is a close-up of the Caravaggio.

12 See Ch. 2.

13 "The secret in life is that everyone must sew it for himself, and … a man can sew it as well as a woman," 74.

14 For *Fear and Trembling* as spectacle (and a diversion from faith), see my *On Søren Kierkegaard*, Ch. 8. Also, see "Seductions and My Carnival Self," above.

15 *Fear and Trembling*, 57.

16 Ibid. This echoes Eckhart. I discuss de silentio's allusion to giving birth to one's father, of being mother to one's father, and hence to oneself, in *Knights of Faith and Resignation: Reading Kierkegaard's Fear and Trembling* (Albany: SUNY, 1996), 40.

17 Jennifer Lemma, a personal note. She adds, "There is an innate philosophical value to Kierkegaard's faith as it pertains to the population of women who are mothers and because of this, it deserves to be recognized as an integral part of ethical, philosophical discourse."

18 See Eric Ziolkowski on Cervantes, *The Literary Kierkegaard* (Evanston: Northwestern, 2011).

19 Yehuda Amichai, *Open Closed Open* (New York: Harcourt, 2000).

20 This is a revision of Edward F. Mooney, Bloomington, Ill. "Difficult Faith and Living Well," in *Kierkegaard's God and the Good Life*, ed. A. Simmons (Indiana University Press, 2017).

Chapter 11

1   *Moby-Dick*, 27.

2   See Herbert Fingarette's *Self-Deception* (Berkeley: University of California Press, 2000)

3   Assertive will stands in the way of letting roots of personal identity reveal their proper salience for embrace: roots in community, family, friendship, and worthy activities.

4   "Human personality," in S. Miles, ed. *Simone Weil: An Anthology* (London: Virago, 2000), 88.

5   Cavell, *Senses of Walden*.

6   I think here of the suicide of Amy Winehouse.

7   Kelly Jolley, personal note.

8   This is the anti-foundationalism of Wittgenstein, Heidegger, and Pragmatism. There can be no requirement that I ground every stance from which I live. Life would then stop dead in its tracks.

9   A revision of Edward F. Mooney. "Kierkegaardian Faith Can't Be Self-Deceptive," in *Kierkegaard and Self-Deception*, ed. Tamar Aylat-Yaguri (Cambridge: Cambridge Scholars Press, 2013).

Chapter 12

1   Nietzsche, *Birth of Tragedy* (London: Penguin, 1994), 22.

2   Job, 14:1–15.

3   This doesn't hold for feminist philosophical criticism since, let us say, 1970.

4   A mother holding a child is prominent in *Fear and Trembling*, and occurs elsewhere, as well. Kierkegaard takes up birth, weaning, and natality, before these become themes for philosophy in the late twentieth century. For him, nursing (and weaning) are also a prerogative of males: "when the child has rested long enough at the mother's breast *it is laid at the father's*, and he too nourishes it with his flesh and blood." *Either/Or* II, trans. Hannay, 388.

5   *Fear and Trembling*, 68–71.

6   An exception is Lucretius "who begins with the mother, with matter itself, with the creative power of matter itself to produce all things." See Andrew Brown, "Mothering Sunday—The maternalizing of matter and the materializing of the mother—a poetic, supreme fiction for our age" posted on his blog *Caute*, 31 March 2019. See also, Psalms Chapter 131:

    1. LORD, my heart is not haughty, nor mine eyes lofty;

    neither do I exercise myself in things too great, or in things too wonderful for me.

    2. *Surely I have stilled and quieted my soul*;

    like a weaned child with his mother; my soul is with me like a weaned child.

7 *Anna Karenina*, Tolstoy, Part 7, 13, many eds.

8 *Feminist Interpretations of Søren Kierkegaard*, ed. Céline Léon and Sylvia Walsh (University Park: Penn State University Press, 1997).

9 "Virility has been the dominant practice such that it is not just the history of events that privileges war; rather the very way we engage intellectually has given priority to death over life." Claire Katz, *Levinas, Judaism, and the Feminine: The Silent Footsteps of Rebecca* (Bloomington: Indiana University Press, 2003), Ch. 10.

10 Gustav Janouch, *Conversations with Kafka* (New York: New Directions, 1971).

11 Climacus turns to a fairy tale parable, "The King and the Maiden," in *Philosophical Crumbs*. He warns that he may not be taken seriously. "Suppose there was a king who loved a maiden of lowly station in life—but the reader may already have lost patience when he hears that our analogy begins like a fairy tale and is not at all systematic." Kierkegaard (2009), 102.

12 Hannay has "Attunement" for the Hongs's "Exordium"; "Speech in Praise of Abraham" for their "Panygeric upon Abraham"; "Preamble from the Heart" for "Preliminary Expectoration."

13 *Silentio* writes a dialectical lyric, knowing that the lyric is apt to conceal the dialectic, and conversely, the dialectic is apt to conceal the lyric. We have something like a decorated set of Russian dolls, each figure opening up to reveal another *smaller* one within, with no end in sight.

14 Johannes *de silentio* gives a "free interpretation" of aspects of Genesis that strike him as crucial. This is not scholarly exegesis committed to the entire story of the binding. Compare Kant: Metaphysical efforts are endeavors "that [we] can never abandon and yet [are] unable to carry to completion." Kant (1965), 295 [A 235–36; B 294–95].

15 *Silentio* writes a dialectical lyric, knowing that lyric is apt to conceal dialectic, and conversely, dialectic is apt to conceal the lyric. We have something like a decorated set of Russian dolls, each wooden figure opening up to reveal another *smaller* one within, with no end in sight.

16 JP VI 6491 (dated 1849).

17 Of course, if we promote Moriah as a Spectacle, we are not investigating faith.

18 *Love's Work* (New York: New York Review Books, 1995), 142.

19 *Fear and Trembling*, 46.

20 Ibid., 45.

21 Ibid., 46.

22 *Fear and Trembling*, 47.

23   From "Birth, Love, and Hybridity: Fear and Trembling" (with Dana Lloyd), *Cambridge Critical Studies, Fear and Trembling*, ed. Dan Conway (Cambridge: Cambridge University Press, 2014).

Chapter 13

1   *Fear and Trembling*, 122.

2   Unrequited love, *Fear and Trembling*, 70.

3   Elsewhere, flute-playing is characterized as a "childish frivolity." *Protagoras*, 347d.

4   212 C.

5   Given Plato's reputed hostility toward poetry (he exiles it from the City in *Republic*) we might assume Socrates will emerge the clear victor in this contest. But Plato's *own* poetry is not exiled: he has a place for image, myth, and parable. He is suspicious of the tragedians, here he floats the possibility of combining tragedy and comedy: so tragic poetry can't be *all* bad.

6   Socrates, neither man nor God, repeats an imperative, "Know thyself," but is not subject to it himself. As the full embodiment of self-knowledge, he is not charged to attain it. Yet if he learns from Diotima, perhaps he *lacks* some self-knowledge.

7   *Fear and Trembling*, 94.

8   Ibid.

9   Ibid.

10 *Fear and Trembling*, 44.

11 *Symposium*, 215b.

12 Ibid., 203c–204a.

13 Ibid., 203c–204a.

14 David M. Halperin, *One Hundred Years of Homosexuality, and Other Essays on Greek Love* (Abingdon: Routledge, 1990), 113.

15 Halperin, *One Hundred Years*, 117.

16 *Symposium*, 206b.

17 *Fear and Trembling*, 57.

18 *Either/Or*, 420.

19 *Love's Work*, 142.

20. Dana Lloyd (Dana Barnea) submitted inspired material on love and hybridity in a Syracuse graduate seminar. I've assimilated her insights into the fabric of my essay, creating a hybridity more dynamic that either of us could have expected. See "Birth, Love, and Hybridity."

Chapter 14

1. *Philosophical Crumbs*: for years the Danish *Smule, Smuler* was translated "Fragments." This suggests assembling fragments into a larger system, or that a larger system has been broken up. "Crumbs" or "trifles" are throwaways. This suggests a lowly *place* in orders of *significance* not something in the order of parts-to-whole. It might also be translated "smidgens."

2. Louis Mackey titles his study *Kierkegaard: A Kind of Poet* (Philadelphia: University of Pennsylvania Press, 1971).

3. Ziolkowski, *The Literary Kierkegaard*.

4. See Friedrich Nietzsche, *The Birth of Tragedy*, trans. Douglas Smith (Oxford: Oxford University Press, 2000), 85 and 93, secs. 15 and 17.

5. Jamie M. Ferreira, *Kierkegaard* (Oxford: Wiley-Blackwell, 2009), 1.

6. The gallery of pseudonyms includes Victor Eremita, Constantin Constantius, Vigilius Haufniensis, and Anti-Climacus, among others. See my "Style and Pseudonymity in Kierkegaard," in *Oxford Handbook to Kierkegaard*, ed. John Lippitt and George Pattison (Oxford: Oxford University Press, 2013), Ch. 10.

7. Ibid.

8. *Prefaces*, 5.

9. Johannes de Silentio's term here. For "Stemning" the Hongs give "Exordium." I prefer Hannay's "Attunement."

10. *Prefaces*, 6.

11. I discuss the enigmas in *Knights of Faith and Resignation: Reading Kierkegaard's Fear and Trembling* (Albany: State University of New York, 1991).

12. Mikhail Bakhtin, *Problems of Dostoevsky's Poetics* (Minneapolis: University of Minnesota Press, 1984).

13. *The Concept of Anxiety*, tr. Walter Lowrie (Princeton, N.J., Princeton University Press, 1944), 42.

14 See Gordon Marino, "The Danish Doctor of Dread," *New York Times*, March 17, 2012.

15 See Robert Pippin, "On 'Becoming Who One Is' (and Failing): Proust's Problematic Selves," in *Philosophical Romanticism*, ed. Nikolas Kompridis (Abingdon: Routledge, 2006), 113–40.

16 See Maurice Merleau-Ponty, *In Praise of Philosophy*, trans. John Wild and James M. Edie (Evanston, Ill.: Northwestern University Press, 1988), 31–39.

17 Ibid. Kelly Dean Jolley develops Merleau-Ponty's discussions of Bergson's decision and links it to the Socratic nature of philosophy in the blog *Quantum Est in Rebus Inane*, August 31, 2012, http://kellydeanjolley.com/2012/08/31/draft-of-mmp-talk/. This was of immense help.

18 From his deathbed, 1854, Kierkegaard writes, "The only analogy I have for what I am doing is Socrates. My task is the Socratic task of revising the definition of what it means to be a Christian." See my *On Søren Kierkegaard*, Chs. 1–3.

19 See "Love, That Lenient Interpreter," in my *On Søren Kierkegaard*, Ch. 5.

20 In my hearing, a colleague held that museums are extensions of colonial aggression, that concert halls are monuments to wealth extracted from the poor, and that writing is a sublimation of sexual desire—nothing more.

21 Jolley, "Merleau-Ponty in Praise of Philosophy," Blog.

22 This is a version of Edward F. Mooney. "Kierkegaard's Disruptions of Literature and Philosophy: Freedom, Anxiety, and Existential Contributions," in *Kierkegaard, Literature, and the Arts*, ed. Eric Zilkowski (Bloomington, Ill.: Northwestern University Press, 2017).

BIBLIOGRAPHY

Alter, Robert. *Genesis: A New Translation*. New York: Norton, 1997.
Amichai, Yehuda. *Open Closed Open*. New York: Harcourt, 2000.
Appalachian Mountain Club White Mountain Guide, 1976 ed., Boston: AMC Books.
Bakhtin, Mikhail. *Problems of Dostoevsky's Poetics*. Minneapolis: University of Minneapolis Press, 1984.
Braver, Lee. "A Brief History of Continental Realism." *Continental Philosophy Review* 23, 2012.
Brown, Andrew. Blog site: *Caute, 31 March 2019* .
Buber, Martin. *Tales of the Hasidim: Later Masters*. New York: Schocken Books, 1948.
Bugbee, Henry. *The Inward Morning, Philosophical Explorations in Journal Form*. New York: Harper and Row, 1976.
Cavell, Stanley. *Little Did I Know: Excerpts from Memory*. Stanford: Stanford University Press, 2010.
Cavell, Stanley. *Must We Mean What We Say: A Book of Essays*. Cambridge: Cambridge University Press, 1976.
Cavell, Stanley. "Passionate and Performative Utterance." In *Contending with Stanley Cavell*, ed. Russell B. Goodman. Oxford: Oxford University Press, 2005.
Cavell, Stanley. *Philosophical Passages, Wittgenstein, Emerson, Austin, Derrida*. New Jersey: Wiley-Blackwell, 1995.
Cavell, Stanley. *Philosophy the Day after Tomorrow*. Cambridge, MA: Harvard University Press, 2005.
Cavell, Stanley. *The Senses of Walden*. Chicago: University of Chicago Press, 1992.
Cavell, Stanley, Cora Diamond, et al. eds. *Philosophy and Animal Life*. New York: Columbia University Press, 2009.
Davenport, John. "Faith as Eschatological Trust in *Fear and Trembling*." In *Ethics, Love, and Faith in Kierkegaard: A Philosophical Engagement*, ed. Edward F. Mooney. Bloomington: Indiana University Press, 2008.
Day, William. "A Soteriology of Reading: Cavell's Excerpts from Memory." In *Stanley Cavell, Literature, and Criticism*, ed. Andrew Taylor. Manchester: Manchester University Press, 2011.
Ferreira, Jamie M. *Kierkegaard*. Oxford: Wiley-Blackwell, 2009.
Fingarette, Herbert. *Self-Deception*. Berkeley: University of California Press, 2000.
Garff, Jaokim. *Søren Kierkegaard: A Biography*, trans. Kirmmse, Bruce. Princeton: Princeton University Press, 2005.
Genesis 50:26. Bible, *New Standard Revised, 1989* .
Glatzner, Nahum, ed. *Dimensions of Job*. New York: Schocken, 1969.

Halperin, David M. *One Hundred Years of Homosexuality, and Other Essays on Greek Love*. Abingdon: Routledge, 1990.
Hannay, Alastair. *Kierkegaard, A Biography*. Cambridge: Cambridge University Press, 2002.
Hauerwas & MacIntyre. *Revisions*. Notre Dame: University of Notre Dame Press, 1983.
Homer. *The Odyssey*, trans. Robert Fagles. New York: Penguin, 1997.
James, William. "The Middle Years." 1893. In *The Tales of Henry James* ed. Edward Wagenknecht. New York: Frederick Ungar, 1984.
Janouch, Gustav. *Conversations with Kafka*. New York: New Directions, 1971.
Jolley, Kelly Dean. Blog *Quantum est in Rebus Inane*, March 22, 2016.
Jolley, Kelly Dean. *Stony Lonesome*. Auburn, AL: New Plains Press, 2014.
Katz, Claire. *Levinas, Judaism, and the Feminine: The Silent Footsteps of Rebecca*. Bloomington: Indiana University Press, 2003.
Kierkegaard, Søren. *Concluding Unscientific Postscript*, trans. Howard and Edna Hong. Princeton, Princeton University Press, 1992.
Kierkegaard, Søren. *Either/Or*, trans. Alastair Hannay. London: Penguin, 1985.
Kierkegaard, Søren. *Fear and Trembling*, trans. Alastair Hannay. London: Penguin, 1985.
Kierkegaard, Søren. *Kierkegaard's Papers and Journals, a Selection*, ed. Alastair Hannay. New York: Penguin, 1996.
Kierkegaard, Søren. *The Sickness Unto Death*, ed and trans. Alastair Hannay, New York, Penguin Books, 1989.
Léon, Céline and Walsh, Sylvia, eds. *Feminist Interpretations of Søren Kierkegaard*. University Park: Penn State University Press, 1997.
Lippitt, John and Pattison, George, eds. *Oxford Handbook to Kierkegaard*. Oxford: Oxford University Press, 2013.
Mackey, Louis. *Kierkegaard: A Kind of Poet*. Philadelphia: University of Pennsylvania Press, 1971.
MacKinnon, D. M. "Death." In *New Essays in Philosophical Theology*, ed. Flew and MacIntyre. New York: St. Martins, 1966.
Marino, Gordon "The Danish Doctor of Dread." *New York Times*. March 17, 2012.
Melville, Herman. *Moby-Dick*. New York: Harper Anniversary Ed., 2001.
Melville, Herman. *Moby-Dick; or, The Whale*, ed. Harrison Hyaford, Hershel Parker, and G. Thomas Tanselle. Evanston: Northwestern University Press, 1988.
Merleau-Ponty, Maurice. *In Praise of Philosophy*, trans. John Wild and James M. Edie. Evanston, Ill.: Northwestern University Press, 1988.
Mooney, Edward F. "Birth, Love, and Hybridity: *Fear and Trembling*" (with Dana Lloyd). In *Cambridge Critical Studies, Fear and Trembling*, ed. Dan Conway. Cambridge: Cambridge University Press, 2014.
Mooney, Edward F. *Excursions with Thoreau: Philosophy, Poetry, Religion*. New York: Bloomsbury, 2017.
Mooney, Edward F. *Knights of Faith and Resignation: Reading Kierkegaard's Fear and Trembling*. Albany: SUNY Press, 1996.
Mooney, Edward F. *Lost Intimacy in American Thought: Recovering Personal Philosophy from Thoreau to Cavell*. London: Continuum, 2009.

Mooney, Edward F. "Love, That Lenient Interpreter." In *On Søren Kierkegaard*. London: Ashgate, 2007.

Mooney, Edward F. *On Søren Kierkegaard: Dialogue, Polemic, Lost Intimacy and Time*. London: Ashgate, 2007.

Mooney, Edward F. "Passion, Reverie, Disaster, Joy: What Philosophers Learn at Sea." In *Melville among the Philosophers*, ed. Corey McCall. Lexington: Lexington Books, 2018.

Mooney, Edward F. "Style and Pseudonyms in Kierkegaard's Authorship," In *Oxford Handbook to Kierkegaard*, ed. John Lippitt and George Pattison. Oxford: Oxford University Press, 2013.

Mooney, Edward F. "Two Testimonies in American Philosophy: Stanley Cavell and Henry Bugbee," *Journal of Speculative Philosophy* 23, 2003.

Mooney, Edward F. *Wilderness and the Heart, Henry Bugbee's Philosophy of Place, Presence, and Memory*. Athens: University of Georgia Press, 2006.

Nietzsche, Friedrich. *The Birth of Tragedy*, trans. Douglas Smith. Oxford: Oxford University Press, 2008.

Pattison, George. "Kierkegaard and the Sublime." In *Kierkegaard Studies Yearbook*. College Park: University of Pennsylvania Press, 1971.

Pippin, Robert. "On 'Becoming Who One Is' (and Failing): Proust's Problematic Selves." In *Philosophical Romanticism*, ed. Nikolas Kompridis. Abingdon: Routledge, 2006.

Plato. *Symposium*. Trans. Walter Hamilton. London: Penguin Classics, 1987.

Randall, John Hermann, "F. H. Bradley and the Working-Out of Absolute Idealism." *Journal of the History of Philosophy* 5, no. 3(July 1967).

Rodick, David. *Wilderness in America*. New York: Fordham, 2017.

Rose, Gillian. *Love's Work*. New York: New York Review Books, 1995.

Rothenberg, David. *Sudden Music: Improvisation, Sound, Nature*. Athens: University of Georgia Press, 2002.

Rudd, Antony. "Wittgenstein and Heidegger as Romantic Modernists." In *Wittgenstein and Heidegger*, ed. Egan et al. Abingdon: Routledge, 2013.

Rushdie, Salmon. *The Ground Beneath Her Feet*. London: Picador, 2000.

Stringfellow, William. *Essential Writings*. Maryknoll, NY: Orbis, 2013.

Weil, Simone, "Human personality." In *Simone Weil: An Anthology*, ed. S. Miles, London: Virago, 2005.

Wittgenstein, Ludwig. *Culture and Value*. Chicago: University of Chicago Press, 1984.

Wittgenstein, Ludwig. *Philosophical Investigations*. London: Blackwell, 1973.

Ziolkowski, Eric. *The Literary Kierkegaard*. Evanston: Northwestern University Press, 2011.

INDEX

Abraham 24, 67–8, 80–4, 103–10, 114–15, 118, 120, 124–6, 137–9, 144
Ahab 45–7, 49, 51, 53–5, 57, 60–3
    twisted stance toward God 53–6
Allen, Woody 142
Amichai, Yehuda 110
    Open Closed Open? 110
Arendt, Hannah 108, 119
Athens 141, 152
attunement 70–71, 107, 123, 126, 144
Auden, W.H. 142
Austen, Jane 122

Bakhtin, Mikhail 144
Barrett, William, *Irrational Man* 23
Beethoven, Ludwig 17–18, 37
belief 36, 63, 70, 76, 89, 92, 104, 118
Bergmann, Ingmar 142
Bergson, Henry 147
birth
    death and 119
    mortality 119–20
    motherhood 121–2
    natality 119–20
Book of Job, The 56
Borgmann, Albert 27, 29
Bradley, F.H. 75
Buber, Martin 77
Bugbee, Henry 7, 27–8, 29–30, 32–5, 38–9, 40
    on Corinthians 29–30
    early life 28
    on Job 30–7
    reminiscence of Cavell, Stanley 38
    sacred and revelatory aspirations 28–9
    specificity of place and time 32–4
    wilderness reflections 38–41
    works

"A Way of Reading Job." 39
Inward Morning: Philosophical Exploration in Journal Form 27–9, 38–40
Sense and Conception of Being, The 37–8

Camus, Albert 23–4
Carnap, Rudolf 29
Cavell, Stanley 2, 4, 6, 38, 48, 115, 161
    King Lear, readings of 38
    on losing self 115
    on passionate speech 2, 4, 6
    poetic philosophies 48
    quotes from Giraudoux, Jean 4, 6
Chorales, Bach 71
Christianity 71, 85, 95, 154. See also religion
    objective view 95
Cixous, Hélène 153

Death. *See specific philosopher's view*
Derrida, Jacques 153, 157
Diamond, Cora 97, 104
Dickinson, Emily 4, 71
Dinesen, Isak 142
Dostoyevsky, *Notes from Underground* 24

Eckhart, Meister 38
Elgar, *Salud D'amour* 101
Eliot, George 5
Emerson, Ralph Waldo 38, 48, 158, 162
Erikson, Erik 24
Evans, Mary Anne. *See also* Eliot, George
    Middlemarch 143
existentialism 23–5, 29, 77. *See also specific philosophers*

American portrayal 24, 29
cultural presence 23
New York Review of Books, essays on 23

faith
multifold 116–17
self awareness and 111–13
self-deception vs 111
transparency 113–16
trust and openness 118
Feminist Interpretations of Søren Kierkegaard 122
Ferreira, Jamie M. 143
Feuerbach, Ludwig 67
First World War 151
Frankfurt, Harry, *Bull Shit* 154
Fromm, Erich 24

God 24–25, 53–5, 60–1, 68, 81–2, 90–1, 98, 104–5, 109–10, 118–20, 126, 134, 138–9
Grimm Brothers, fairy tales 15

Halperin, David M. 135–6
Hannay, Alastair 14
Hegel, G.W.F. 77, 88, 115
Phenomenology 20
religious views 67
Scientific System 15
Heidegger, Martin 9–11, 20, 75, 77, 108, 142, 158
on passionate speech 9
Hocking, W.E. 2
Homer 15–16, 80
The Odyssey 15, 22

Ibsen, Henrik 77, 142
immortality 45, 54, 56, 64–5, 100, 135, 154
Ishmael 44, 46–8, 50–1, 53, 56–7–9, 63–5, 161–2
as birth name 57
critique of Ramadan 51
rebirth and renewal 57–8

James, Henry 5, 7, 27–8
Jaspers, Karl 77

Jolley, Kelly Dean 1, 40, 149, 167 n.18, 168 n.12, 172 n17, 179 n.17
Stony Lonesome 164 n.1

Kafka, Franz 77, 123, 142
Kant, Immanuel 12, 45, 48, 72–3, 81, 90, 92, 105, 166 n.6, 176 n.14
Karamazov, Alyosha 71
Kaufmann, Walter, *Existentialism from Dostoevsky to Sartre* 23
Kierkegaard, Søren
on absolute paradox 88–9
on apocalyptic anxieties 24–5
on birth and rebirth 108, 119
carnivalesque textual style 126–7
Christian, view on 67, 71
comparison to Socrates 141
creativity 15–16
on death and birth 139
on divine grounding power 92–3
early life 77
on essence of humanity 90–1
existentialism 14, 77, 79, 85, 99, 102, 144–9
faithful living 103–4
on four strings of identity 96–8, 100–1
graveyard scene 71–4
human existence, three stage theory 79
hybridity dynamics 131–5
on indirect communication 88–9
on living through difficult reality. 104–8
on love and passion 129–30, 135–7
lyric and dialectics 122–4
mentors 78
multiple interpretations 98
presence of words and delivery 10–11
pseudonym
Bene, Nicholas Note 143
Climacus, Johannes 14–16, 19, 21, 71–3, 78, 80, 84, 91, 143, 145–6
silentio, Johannes de 67–8, 78, 80, 82, 93, 105–9, 120–1, 123, 127, 129–31, 133, 136–9, 142–3, 171 n.3, 174 n.16, 176 n.14

religious ideas 74–6, 80–3, 88–9, 109–10, 152
on role of knowledge in life 11–12, 77–8
self, notion of 74–6, 90–1
subjectivity of truth 9, 69, 72, 76, 86
on truth 72, 85–6, 153
volatile mix of character 142–3
on weaning mothers 121, 124–6, 137–9
well-lived life, concept of 103
works
    Concept of Anxiety, The 84, 145, 178 n.13
    Concept of Irony with Constant Reference to Socrates, The 86–8
    Concluding Unscientific Postscript to Philosophical Crumbs: A Mimic-Pathetic-Dialectic Compilation-an Existential Contribution 11–14, 16, 19–22, 71, 75, 78, 84–6, 100, 107, 141–6
    "Dialectical Lyric" 67
    "Diary of the Seducer" 79, 95, 141
    Either/Or 78–80, 84, 99–101, 141–3, 175 n.4
    Epigraph 109
    Fear and Trembling 12–13, 24, 68, 78, 80–2, 84, 92, 98, 100, 103, 106–8, 113, 115, 120, 122, 124–5, 129–31, 141–3, 173 n.10, 175 n.4
    A Final Unscholarly Afterthought, Sequel to Scraps of Philosophy: A Mimicking, Pathos-filled, Dialectical Compendium, an Existential Provocation. 100–1
    "The Musical Erotic" on Mozart's *Don Giovanni* 79
    Philosophical Crumbs: a Mimic Pathetic Dialectical Compilation: an Existential Contribution 13–14, 21, 80, 84–5, 107, 141–2, 144, 176 n.11, 178 n.1
    Point of View of My Work as an Author, The 7
    Prefaces 85, 100–1, 143–4
    Problema 109
    Repetition 12, 78, 83–4, 90, 100
    Sickness unto Death 89–90
    Speech in Praise of Abraham 109
    Stages on Life's Way 79, 141–2
    writing style 9–10, 80–1, 84–5, 98–102, 106–8, 122–4
knowledge 6, 11–12, 40, 77–8, 113, 115, 129, 137–8, 145

Lewis, C. I. 29
life/living philosophy
    Bugbee's view 27, 34, 39, 41
    CAUTION 1–4, 6
    Christian 15
    death and 25
    difficult realities 47
    Kant's view 72
    Kierkegaard on tang of life 9, 11–15, 17, 22, 24, 61, 63–4, 75–6, 78–80, 82–8
    Marino on 25–6
    Melville's view 47–8
    well-lived 103, 110

Marcel, Gabriel, *Metaphysical Journals* 28
Marino, Gordon 23–6
    on existential dimensions of living 25–6
    Existentialist's Survival Guide: How to Live Authentically in an Inauthentic Age 23, 26
    view on psychology and philosophy 24
May, Rollo 24
McKinnon, D. M. 47
Melville, Herman 7, 38, 43–4, 46–9, 56, 59, 62, 65, 111, 161
    on birth 57–8, 63
    on death 57–8, 61, 63–4
    Genesis 57–8
    on natural world 49–50
    on racial and religious diversity 59–60
    on rebirth 57–8, 63

on truth 46–7, 59, 62–3
whale, depiction of 43–6, 48, 50, 55–9, 63–5, 153
works
   Moby-Dick 43, 45, 53, 55–7, 59
   sea tales 58–63
Montaigne 11, 48
   Essays 7
Moore, G.E. 29

Nietzsche, Friedrich 24, 47–8, 67, 77, 89, 142, 152–3
   Birth of Tragedy 175 n.1, 178 n.4

Old Testament 45
Ortega, José 77, 142

Partisan Review 23
Pattison, George 91–2
Philosophy. *See also* life/living philosophy
   American 27–8
   Anglophone 27, 41
   episodic 43, 47, 50
   European 145
   formal 44
   modern 48
Plato 10–11, 11, 38, 50–1, 129–30, 133, 136–7, 139
   Symposium 51, 129
prayer 30, 69, 154–5, 162–3
Putnam 29

Quine, W. V. O. 27, 29

Rawls, John, *A Theory of Justice* 27
religion 3, 8, 20, 30, 43, 47, 51, 67–8, 75–8, 109, 160
   intimacy and subjectivity 69–71
religious sensibility 67–71, 75–76, 160, 162
Rilke 24, 77, 98, 142
Rorty, Richard 154
Rose, Gillian 124, 138
Rothenberg, David 2
Rousseau'
   Emily 122
   Reveries of a Solitary Walker 7

Royce, Josiah 27–8
Rushdie, Salmon 17–18
Russell, Bertrand 29
Ryle, Gilbert 29

Sartre, Jean-Paul 24, 77, 97, 142, 172 n.3
Schopenhauer, Arthur 11, 46, 152
Second World War 27, 38, 151
Shakespeare, William 29, 38, 170 n.10
Smith, Huston 29
Socrates 46, 68, 78, 81, 85–8, 92–3, 122, 126, 129–39, 141–2, 146–7, 149
Spinoza, Baruch 38, 48
Stein, Gertrude 157
Stevens, Wallace 155
subjectivity 6, 20, 48, 69–71, 78, 86, 149, 159

Thoreau, Henry David 27, 29, 38, 47–8, 155, 158, 162
   Journals 28
   on truth 155
Tillich, Paul 77
Tolstoy, Leo 71
   Death of Ivan Ilyich, The 24–5, 71
trust 16, 18, 83, 104–6, 108, 114, 118, 132, 158
truth
   religious 160–3
   tactile 158–60
   theory of 155–8

Updike, John 142

Village Voice, The 23

Weil, Simone 115
wisdom 7, 13, 29–30, 40, 47, 60, 68, 127, 130, 134–5, 137
Wittgenstein, Ludwig 4, 11, 21, 48, 75, 142–3, 147, 151–4, 158, 165 n.5, 167 n.18, 172 n.15, 175 n.8
   Austrian roots 151–2
   on Kierkegaard 152
   on truth 151–3

Zen philosophy 29, 89